Gilbert Milligan Tucker

Our common speech: six papers on topics connected with the proper use of the English language, the changes which that tongue is undergoing on both sides of the sea

Gilbert Milligan Tucker

Our common speech: six papers on topics connected with the proper use of the English language, the changes which that tongue is undergoing on both sides of the sea

ISBN/EAN: 9783337220419

Hergestellt in Europa, USA, Kanada, Australien, Japan

Cover: Foto ©Suzi / pixelio.de

Weitere Bücher finden Sie auf **www.hansebooks.com**

OUR COMMON SPEECH:

SIX PAPERS

ON TOPICS CONNECTED WITH THE PROPER USE
OF THE ENGLISH LANGUAGE,
THE CHANGES WHICH THAT TONGUE IS UNDER-
GOING ON BOTH SIDES OF THE SEA,
AND THE LABORS OF LEXICOGRAPHERS TO EX-
PLAIN THE MEANING OF THE WORDS
OF WHICH IT IS COMPOSED.

BY

GILBERT M. TUCKER.

NEW YORK:
DODD, MEAD AND COMPANY.
1895.

𝔘niversity 𝔓ress:
JOHN WILSON AND SON, CAMBRIDGE, U.S.A.

CONTENTS.

OUR COMMON SPEECH.

———•———

LOCUTIUS IN FABRICA.

Words are those Channels, by which the Knowledge of Things are conveyed to our Understandings: and therefore, upon a right Apprehension of them depends the Rectitude of our Notions; and in order to form our Judgments right, they must be understood in their proper Meaning, used in their true Sense, either in Writing or Speaking: For, if the Words of the Speaker or Writer, though ever so apposite to the Matter, be taken in a wrong Sense, they form erroneous Ideas in the Mind concerning the Thing spoken or written of; and if we use Words in a false and improper Sense, this causes Confusion in the Understanding of the Hearer, and renders the Discourse unintelligible. — *Introduction to Bailey's Dictionary*.

IN an office-building which I occasionally visit, is a dingy little room occupied as a shop by one of those useful men who can turn their hands to almost any mechanical task, from repairing a fine clock to building a cow-shed, and do it well. To the casual observer, the place is far from beautiful, and has a "cluttered-up" appearance, suggestive of habits the reverse of orderly. The floor — where not occupied by benches, lathes, horses, and a rusty stove surmounted by a glue-kettle — is nearly concealed by bits of timber, shavings, and miscellaneous débris. The walls are lined with shelves and racks of many shapes, sizes and colors, obviously put up at different times, and constructed of odds and ends, with no thought of symmetry or harmony in their arrangement. And when one examines the tools themselves, they are found to form a collection almost equally promiscuous. No two have handles alike, or look as if they came from the same maker. They are disposed in rude stands, boxes and cases of irregular forms, which seem to have been hastily adapted to their present purpose, in default of anything better. Nothing could be more unlike the finely finished and ingeniously arranged "gentlemen's tool-chests" that fascinate the eye of mechanically-disposed visitors in hardware stores.

Yet the occupant of this little shop can lay his hand in a moment on any article in it, by day or by night, and knows the contents as you know the alphabet. And when he puts any implement into service, it is found to answer its purpose to very perfection. The chisels cut like razors; the saws follow the line without the deflection of a hair's-breadth; the lathes run exactly true; the vices and clamps hold like a bad habit. For all their rude appearance, it would be hard to suggest any improvement in the practical working of this collection of heterogeneous apparatus.

Now, I have often thought, while watching this mechanic at work, that his position (barring, of course, any question as to relative degrees of skill) is in some respects not unlike that of the writer of an English book. Is not our language, too, a seemingly disordered and inharmonious assemblage of implements, appliances and raw material? Our vocabulary is made up of importations from every country under heaven; our present tenses and their preterites, our individual terms and their significance in idiomatic phrases, our spoken words

and their representatives in writing, have in
scores of·cases about as much seeming congruity as my mechanical friend's delicate watch-
making lathe with the dirty table on which it
stands and the rough box that covers it. And
yet, what work can be accomplished with the
English language! What distinction so fine,
what conception so grand, what mental creation
so lovely, that this unsymmetrical and in many
respects unbeautiful tongue is inadequate (if
one only knows how to use it) for putting it
into permanent form for preservation? As a
means for the expression of thought, our common speech, in the hands of a master, excels
the comparatively regular languages of antiquity and of many savage peoples, as the
mechanic's unattractive tools excel for practical
purposes the handsome but untrustworthy contents of the "gentlemen's tool-chests." Less
sonorous than German, less sparkling than
French, less musical than Spanish, less logical
and systematic by far in its structure than
Latin, less flexible than Greek, how it surpasses
them all for meeting the varied necessities of
mankind!

Now, does not this parallelism suggest a useful lesson to certain hypercritical critics whose wont it is to act the part of grand inquisitors as to the legitimacy of the new terms which are constantly appearing in our language, often to supply real and important wants? A great hubbub was made by this class of people on the introduction of the now well-established noun *starvation*, which even Mr. Skeat, notwithstanding his usual liberality of judgment, condemns as a "ridiculous hybrid." Hybrid of course it is, — an Anglo-Saxon root with a Latin suffix; as if one should fit a rough hickory handle into a highly polished lignum-vitæ mallet. But, ridiculous? Consider the circumstances. The implement was badly needed; the materials of which it was constructed were the best at hand at the moment, or the best that were thought of; and it answers its purpose well. Can we afford to discard it because it is not handsome in appearance? *Reliable* has fallen under the ban of the same class of thinkers. It *is* badly formed, no doubt; but so, for that matter, is its parent, the universally accepted verb *rely*, and still more so the unchal-

lenged noun *reliance*, consisting as this does of
an English root with a French prefix and suffix,
like an old, well-worn spoke-shave with a pair of
bran-new handles. (As to the other objection
to *reliable*, — that we do not *rely a thing*, but *rely
upon it*, and therefore the adjective ought to be
rely-upon-able, — any comment may safely be
deferred until people begin saying *laugh-at-able*,
indispense-with-able, and *unaccount for-able ;* the
principle is the same.) Fault is perpetually
found with *talented*, on the ground that participles ought not to be formed from nouns; and
perhaps they ought not, in a strictly logical
and regular language; but a tongue that already includes *diseased, gifted, lettered, bigoted,
turreted, landed, skilled, ivied, crannied, towered,
blooded, cultured, acred, steepled, mitred, coped,
tippeted, booted, spurred, horned, unprincipled* and
widowed (not to mention innumerable compounds like *fair-haired* and *pug-nosed*), will
hardly suffer much by admitting other forma-
tions of the same kind. The process is continuing, and is bound to continue. A recent
instance may be found in the cable despatch to
the American press conveying the news of the

death of the last Duke of Marlborough. "The dukedom," said the despatch, "will be the heaviest-*dowagered* title in the peerage." The mere fact that these noun-participles are so freely formed and so generally accepted is almost enough to establish their standing as good English, without argument; in the formation of a language, whatever generally is, is right. But I think it may be successfully maintained that the objectors are wrong in their argument, too, for these participles, in fact, are regularly formed from a noun *used as a verb*, in accordance with what seems to be a fundamental law of the language, that *any noun, without exception, may be used as a verb whenever such use is necessary or convenient.* Of course thousands of our nouns never have been, probably never will be, so used, — either because they have well established related verbs that answer the purpose; or because considerations of euphony make it natural to turn them into the verb form by adding *ize* or making some other modification, when it is desired to make verbs of them; or because their meanings are such that they are never wanted except as nouns. But I believe the law

of liberty above stated will more and more com-
mend itself as sound, the more it is tested by
experiment.[1]

Not to protract the list of words that have
been condemned because of their real or supposed irregularity of formation, we will only
notice the class of which *stand-point*, *wash-tub*,
shoe-horn, *cook-stove*, *go-cart* and *boot-jack* are
examples, — a class of words which are set down
as abominations, "slovenly and uncouth," by a
popular writer on correctness in speech, because
they do not conform in their structure to a
somewhat complicated canon which he lays
down as the law for making " compounds of
this kind." His argument is a complete non-
sequitur. The laws relating to the development of a language are to be deduced from
the history of that development, just as the
so-called laws of nature are merely generalised
statements of observed facts. And in regard

---

[1] Of course it does not follow that any English verb may be
used as a noun. No such practice has ever prevailed ; no such
practice is necessary or desirable for useful ends ; and any
attempt to introduce it — as in creating monsters like "a combine " — deserves to be excommunicated with bell, book and
candle.

to these expressions, which our acceptance of
his canon would require us to condemn, it
must be noticed that they are not only briefer
(always an advantage), but actually clearer than
those which the critic would substitute for them.
The meaning of a *cooking-stove*, to be sure, is
not greatly liable to misapprehension, nor perhaps is that of a *washing-tub;* but *booting-jack*
is open to the manifest objection that it is not
for booting, but for un-booting, so to speak,
that the implement is designed, while *shoeing-
horn* suggests an entirely wrong idea: we do
not speak of the process of dressing our feet
as "shoeing" them; and what sort of a description of the well-known nursery machine
would it be to call it a "going-cart"?

The fact of the matter seems to be that
though of course it is desirable that the development of the language should proceed on
regular lines and in conformity with logical
principles, it is by no means essential to the
usefulness of a word that it should be thus
formed; and if only the word is useful, we
can well afford to admit it to our already heter-   -
ogeneous vocabulary, the vocabulary being all

the more serviceable in many ways on account
of the variety and lack of unity among its constituent parts. The important question in all
such cases, looking at them from the mechanical point of view, is, have we need of this tool,
and is it the best we can readily procure? If
so, we shall be just so much the poorer for re-
jecting it on account of its uncouth appearance.

It ought to be remembered, indeed, that our
list of words, numerous as it is, is yet not comprehensive enough to fulfill the highest ideal
of a perfect tongue. We need more tools, —a
good many of them; and it sometimes seems
a pity rather that we cannot manufacture and
introduce them when the need is perceived,
than that some of those we have, offend in
their composition the strict requirements of
congruity. We badly need, for instance, epi-
cene pronouns in the singular, answering to
they, *them* and *their* in the plural. True it is,
one can often use *he*, *him*, and *his*, expecting
hearers or readers to remember that "the
brethren embrace the sistern." True it also
is, one can often get around the difficulty by
rearranging a sentence; but there *is* a diffi-

culty, for all that. A man wishes to say that each of his two children, a boy and a girl, has the exclusive use of a desk. He náturally begins: " Each of my children has a desk to " — how shall he finish? It is not quite right to say that each has a desk to *himself,* or to *herself,* and it is certainly far from grammatical or pleasing to say *themselves.* What shall he do? The problem is of daily occurrence, as any one will find who will take pains to watch for it.

We need, too, a preterite for the verb *must,* and still more for the verb *ought.*[1] We are compelled to say, " You ought to have done such and such things," — which is by no means what we really mean. One cannot possibly be under obligation to *have done* anything, — the phrase is absurd; all obligation is *to do,* and it would be an important gain in the direction of clearness and conciseness if we might say, when speaking of past time, " you oughted."

We need, again, a word almost synonymous with *many,* but having a slightly different shade

[1] Each of these words was itself anciently a preterite; but they have been for centuries independent verbs, used only in a single tense, the present indicative.

of meaning, — a lack which is often supplied, awkwardly and incorrectly, by the use of *numerous* with a plural noun. People say, "There are numerous books on that subject," — which is hardly grammatical: there may be a numerous *list* of books, but that expression, correct in syntax, does not seem quite to express the idea; and to say there are *many* books may be rather too strong a statement.

We need, once more, a verb for which *replace* is commonly substituted, there being nothing better at hand. One removes a painting from his wall and hangs up an engraving in its stead. For a brief statement of this action, we have at present nothing better than to say that the painting was replaced by the engraving. Yet this is really nonsense. To replace a thing is to put it back where it was before. Here, as in the case of *numerous*, we may be said to lack a gimlet, and find ourselves compelled to bore holes, blunderingly and unsatisfactorily, with the blade of a penknife.

Then there are not a few adverbs which one meets in foreign tongues, and finds so useful that he wonders at himself for never having noticed the absence of corresponding words in English. Familiar examples are *freundlich* and *hoffentlich* in German. One cannot say in English, "He received me friendlily," convenient as it would sometimes be to do so, neither *kindly* nor *cordially* quite answering the purpose. Nor can one say, "The doctor has hopeably given the right medicine." If you presume he has done so, you may say *presumably;* if you are sure of it, you have *undoubtedly;* but if you only desire to express a pretty strong hope, you must cast your sentence in another mould.

At the same time, we have certainly bad words enough, — bad, not because they are irregular in form or composed of incongruous elements, but because they are, for some other reason (adopting Noah Webster's sententious expression), "nonsensical." *Helpmeet* is one of these monsters. The result of a stupid blunder in running together a noun and an adjective that stand separate in the familiar verse in Genesis, it can hardly be called a word at all; it means nothing in particular, and is worse than useless. *Dissever, disannul, unravel, lesser,*

and similar feeble attempts at unnecessary emphasis, are other instances: *sever, annul, ravel,
less*, answer the purpose completely, with the
advantage of smaller bulk; the addition of the
extra syllable is like giving a gimlet two handles.
Equally useless, for the most part, is the school-
ma'amish insistence upon indicating, by the
addition of *ess*, the feminine gender in a number of nouns indicative of occupation or position.   Sometimes, of course, the sex of the
person referred to has a direct bearing upon
her relations to her calling, as in the case of
an actress, whom it is often doubtless well to
discriminate, in speech as in thought, from an
actor.   But it can hardly be maintained that
any such necessity exists in the case of a
woman who may happen to be an editor, a
postmaster, a manager, or a poet.   Yet we read
not unfrequently of editresses and postmis-
tresses; the dignified " Westminster Review "
finds *poet* not sufficiently distinct when the poet is
a woman, and gives its sanction to *poetess;* and
the " Illustrated London News," which often de-
votes a considerable portion of one of its most
entertaining departments to discussions of col-

loquial English, its meaning and its proprieties, is actually guilty of *manageress !* Here, as before, the extra syllable is merely an incumbrance; we could not only get along just as well without it, we should actually do better.

Another class of bad words — bad because they do not mean what they are supposed to mean — is exemplified in *gasometer*. The fact that it consists of a term invented in Belgium not much more than two hundred years ago, and a word from classical Greek, welded together, nobody knows why, by the letter *o*, — is of no consequence; but what is of consequence is, that it means a measurer of gas, and is understood as indicating a reservoir of gas. In the name of common-sense, when one means a gas-holder, why not say so ? *Hydropathy*, too, is a disgrace to the language. *Homœopathy* (similar sickness) is correct, indicating as it does a method of treatment based on the belief that " like cures like ; " and *allopathy* (different sickness), though of course rather a nickname than a scientific term, may pass muster as designating the practice that commonly relies on agencies which are found to *reverse* the symptoms of the patient. *Hydropathy* (water sickness) can only be accounted for by supposing that the inventor of the word imagined that it might mean water-*cure*, which of course it cannot.

But by far the most important suggestion offered by the analogies of the little shop, relates to the folly of *misusing* our verbal tools; and just here is the one great point of dissimilarity between the English language and the equipment of my friend's workroom. A mallet may be highly polished as to its head, and roughhewn as to its handle, and yet give entire satisfaction. But it would hardly work well on chisels, if the owner were in the habit of using it to drive nails. That is exactly what we not unfrequently do in speech; and the natural result follows: the nails are not driven straight, and we presently find that we have spoiled our mallet. A few examples will make the process clear.

We speak of *preposterous* statements, meaning only that they are *incorrect* or *absurd*. Now, *preposterous* is not properly synonymous with either of these adjectives, but has a definite import of its own which can be expressed by no other word, signifying as it does the putting of something first which ought to be last, — the getting of the cart before the horse, as it were. We are badly compensated for losing the power of expressing this idea in a single word, by gaining a new and hardly distinguishable synonym for *absurd*.

Then there is *aggravating* for *exasperating*. The distinction has been pointed out a thousand times. Everybody knows that to aggravate is to make worse. A man's crime may be aggravated by the circumstances; to say that the man himself is aggravated, means, not that he is annoyed, but that, being an evil at best, he is made a greater nuisance than he has been. Yet it is surprising how many influential writers, especially in England, insist on confounding the terms. Dickens does so over and over again in " Great Expectations ": " The Romans must have aggravated one another very much with their noses; " " Mr. Wopsle's Roman nose aggravated me; " " This was so very aggravating, the more especially as I found myself making no way against his surly obtuseness; "

"Words cannot state the amount of aggrava-
tion and injury wreaked upon me by Trabb's
boy." I read the other day in the "Mark Lane
Express" of persons who "jerk the reins in
that aggravating manner." A pamphlet lately
published in London, relating to a certain class
of books in the British Museum, is entitled
"Aggravating Ladies." The careful "Westminster Review" says (October, 1881, page
284, Scott edition), "The selections from the
'Giaour' are exceedingly aggravating." It must,
however, be admitted that the blunder is not
exclusively British, for whoever reads that excellent book, "The Calling of a Christian
Woman," issued a few years ago by the Rev.
Morgan Dix, S. T. D., rector of Trinity Church,
New York, will find on page 22 a reference to
"the words of St. Paul peculiarly aggravating
to the ears of modern revolutionists."

A mallet which has been so persistently used
as a hammer by the legal profession, without
sense or necessity, as to be pretty effectually
ruined, is *enjoin*. It can hardly be needful
to remark that to enjoin a course of conduct is
to command that it be followed; the lawyers,

oddly enough, have so perverted the meaning
as to reverse it completely; in their dialect, to
enjoin an act is to forbid it! Thus I read in the
" Albany Law Journal " (vol. xxviii. page 43) that
" in *Leete* v. *Pilgrim Church*, St. Louis Court of
Appeals, the ringing of church chimes between
9 P. M. and 7 A. M. was enjoined. The court
refused to enjoin the ringing for worship on
Sunday or in the daylight hours, and continued :
' But the striking of the clock at night must, we
think, be relegated to the category of useless
noises. . . . We therefore think that the striking of the hours upon the largest bell between
the hours of 9 P. M. and 7 A. M. ought to be
enjoined ' " ! Of course this means that while
the court declined to order the ringing of the
church bell on Sunday or by daylight during
the week, it did command that the chimes
should be faithfully operated between nine at
night and seven in the morning. Of course
also the writer of the paragraph, and the learned
judge who prepared the opinion, intended that
their words should mean the precise opposite.
The mallet in their hands is absolutely spoiled
for its legitimate purpose; and to what possible

profit ? Meaning *forbidden*, why could they
not say *forbidden ?* Or if it is considered desirable to have a special word to signify the formal
forbidding of an action by a writ, far, far better
would it be to raise to respectability a term
which is now ranked with the vilest newspaper
slang, and say that the action is "injuncted."
It may be answered that this horrible word, if
it means anything, must be synonymous with
enjoin; but the fact is, it has never been used
except to signify *forbidden by injunction;* and
as for its irregular formation, one who cares
more for the substance of the language, its real
serviceableness in expressing thought, than for
the refinements of grammatical science, will
easily disregard that objection. The nail must
be driven ; the only hammer we have is "forbid: " this, it seems, will not answer ; then for
Heaven's sake let us pick up even a shape-
less stone like "injunct" rather than spoil our
excellent mallet "enjoin."[1]

---

[1] A portion of this paragraph was printed in the "Albany
Law Journal" (with editorial commendation) shortly after the
publication of the legal opinion criticized, and elicited a number
of indignant letters from lawyers, not one of which really

Among the great number of other verbal mallets which are often foolishly misused as hammers, the following may be mentioned.

attacked the position above assumed. Their chief burden was to maintain that a man may properly be *enjoined from* doing a certain action, — which nobody disputed; the question (if there can be any question) is, whether one may say that "*the action* is enjoined," meaning that the action is forbidden. One writer stated that "neither the verb 'to enjoin' nor its substantive 'injunction' is *exclusively* used, even in legal phraseology, in the sense of prohibition;" nobody said it was: the point is, that it ought *never* to be so used. Another solemnly quoted — of all authorities in the world, on a question of verbal accuracy — *Webster's Dictionary!* — as if everybody did not know that all kinds of error in speech which have obtained any sort of respectable currency can be defended (not "*authorised*") by citations from that useful but bloated compilation. The editor of the "Law Journal," closing the discussion, summed up the whole matter thus : "What Mr. Tucker complains of is that the same word is used to mean two exactly opposite things, — to do and not to do. This verbal blowing hot and cold in the same breath is certainly indefensible. It is 'overworking' the verb, to quote Rufus Choate. We have plenty of good words to express the desired meaning, — 'prohibit,' 'restrain,' 'forbid.' There is no need of corrupting and vulgarising the language by this double and ambiguous use. When we want to prohibit the ringing of bells, for example, let us not say it is 'enjoined,' *i. e.*, commanded; nor worse yet, 'enjoined and forbidden,' *i. e.*, both commanded and prohibited; but let us say just what we mean in the correct use of the language, — forbidden and prohibited. We are no purist nor

The list might be indefinitely extended, but it is the present purpose merely to illustrate the principle.

Restive for *uneasy*. — Here is a word which shares with *enjoin* the remarkable misfortune of having been completely reversed in meaning by bad usage. A restive horse is a lazy horse that wants to rest, and by no means, as sometimes seems to be supposed, a nervous horse that wants to go.

Executive for *secret*, in the phrase " executive session." It is generally understood that when

---

'philological fancier,' but we think that this use of the word 'enjoin' is radically wrong."

The practical result of the bad practice is strikingly illustrated by an article which appeared in a Morgantown, W. Va., newspaper, the " New Dominion," of April 14, 1894, to which a friend calls attention as these pages are going to press. Relating a decision of the Supreme Court (presumably of the State) in the case of *Lewis Wilson* v. *The Town of Philippi*, the syllabus of the opinion is quoted as saying that under certain circumstances " a court of equity will not enjoin the collection of a tax assessment on a town lot to pay for the construction of a sidewalk in front of the same, ordained by the council of an incorporated city or town." The reader perceives, of course, that it is impossible to know, except by inference from the context, whether *enjoin* here means *command* or *forbid!*

the Senate engages in what is properly enough
called "executive business," as the consideration of appointments or treaties, spectators are
excluded; and from this has arisen a ridiculous
custom on the part of various voluntary associa-
tions and committees of resolving to "go into
executive session" when it is only meant that
private business is to be taken up with closed
doors. The blunder is doubtless largely due to
the usual preference of ill-trained minds for fine
and high-sounding words.

Condign for *severe.* — *Condign* means *suitable;*
and the most trifling offences, if serious enough
to require attention at all, should incur *condign*
punishment just as truly as the greatest crimes.

Fabulous for *very great.* — One may properly
speak of the fabulous wealth of an impostor,
meaning the property that he falsely pretends
to have. But what nonsense it is, when one
thinks of it, to say that a lady's jewels are of
"fabulous value," meaning that they cost a
great deal of money!

Impertinent for *insolent.* — An impertinent
remark is one that has no connection with the
matter under discussion. But the use of the

term ought not to be thought to imply any
censure on the good manners of the speaker
referred to, for the most courteous person in the
world makes an impertinent remark whenever
he introduces a new topic of conversation. To
call the person " impertinent," in any case, is to
" mix things " badly. A person can no more
be " impertinent " than he can be irrelevant or
disconnected.

Temperance, Sumptuary, and *Protective.* —
Without expressing any opinion as to the
advisability of indulging in alcoholic beverages,
one may properly denounce, from grammatical
considerations only, the absurdity of speaking
of a man who abjures them entirely, as " strictly
temperate," and the absurdity of characterising
as " sumptuary " the legislation which aims to
regulate the sale of intoxicants. A man cannot
be " temperate " with that which he does not
use ; and " sumptuary " laws, which forbid men
under certain circumstances to make certain
purchases, — being intended for the financial
benefit of the persons on whom they bear, —
differ by the whole diameter of being from the
laws about liquor-selling, which are not intended

at all for the benefit of the class to whom they apply, but are designed to restrict the injury which these men inflict upon others. And similarly, without expressing any opinion as to the wisdom of a national policy of limiting importations from foreign countries, one may point out that the name "protective tariff," as applied to a tariff by which this result is brought about, is objectionable, for the reason that it begs the whole question at issue. Such a tariff *restricts, limits*. Whether it really *protects* anything, in any proper application of the term, is disputed.

Dividend. — It may be worth while to call attention to the obvious fact that a dividend is that which is to be divided. A railroad's dividend, for instance, is a certain share of the profits, set aside by the directors for division among the stockholders. It is sometimes convenient, of course, and perhaps not highly censurable, to speak of one of the proprietors as receiving "his dividend," meaning his *share of* the dividend; but it should be remembered that this expression is only justifiable as a rough sort of contraction, much like saying "governments"

and "railroads" when one means government
bonds and railroad securities; and it is to be
regretted that the definition of *dividend* in each
of the two dictionaries most in use in this
country is so worded as apparently to confuse
dividend with *quotient.* Webster's, as usual, is a
little worse than Worcester's.

Circumstance for *event.* — We continually hear
people say that they will " relate a circumstance
that occurred " under their own observation. A
circumstance occur! They might as well speak
of the motionless scenery at a theatre as per-
forming. The word properly used — to indicate
(as the Latin grammars used to say of the abla-
tive absolute) the " time, cause or concomitants
of an action, or the condition on which it
depends " — was extremely useful, and we are
very poorly compensated for its loss by acquir-
ing a new and hardly distinguishable synonym
for " *event* " or " *incident.*"

Demean for *debase.* — " If you had once demeaned yourself, what I have to say would
come easy," says Gwen in " A Yellow Aster."
The person addressed had demeaned himself
(well or badly) every moment of his waking

hours, all his life. The blunder seems to have
arisen partly from an imagined relationship between the verb *demean* and the adjective *mean*,
and partly from the fact that the verb is used in
a good many rather familiar passages in old and
standard writers, in such connection that *debase*
would have made equally good sense. Recol-
lection of the noun *demeanor*, which is certainly
not synonymous with *debasement*, ought to be
sufficient to correct the error.

Merchant for *tradesman* or *shopkeeper.* — In
the older and better use of the first word, it was
strictly confined to persons who carried on foreign traffic. To call retail dealers " merchants "
is to multiply synonyms uselessly, at the cost of
losing a very convenient distinction.

Sustain for *receive.* — Chiefly in daily-paper
language; "the victim sustained a trifling bruise
on his arm." Well, it would have been remarkable if he had *not* " sustained " a wound
of that description. The writer was, of course,
trying to say that the person *received* the
wound. How hard it is, sometimes, to be
simple !

Liable for *likely.* — A wrongdoer is liable to

punishment. To say that he is "liable to escape," meaning that he is *likely* to escape, is to commit an error that is really comical in its absurdity, when one compares the true meaning of the sentence with the idea intended to be conveyed. The error, nevertheless, creeps sometimes into very good company. Julian Hawthorne is guilty of it — see "Dust," chapter 7, page 62 of Fords, Howard & Hulbert edition of 1883 : "Perdita was brought up as befitted a young lady liable to hold a good position in society." The "Albany Law Journal" quotes, vol. 29, page 22, from an official English report, an account of a meeting " of all the judges liable to try prisoners."

Monopoly. — The frequent and glaring misuse of this term is of no little importance, as it leads to confusion of thought and sometimes to very ill-advised political action. A monopoly is, of course, an industry that is protected from competition by legal enactment. Certain demagogues are doing their best to lead the unthinking multitude to apply the term to industries which are perfectly open to competition but in which, for one reason or another, nobody

cares to compete — a very widely different
thing. The owner of a patent has a monopoly;
but the notion that railroading, banking or gas-
making can be a monopoly, as long as all the
world is at liberty to engage therein if it pleases,
is at once grotesque and dangerous.

The list stretches out indefinitely; one knows
not where to stop. It seems that on this
subject, as on some others, there is verily need
of line upon line, precept upon precept, here
a little and there a good deal. Yet one word
of caution must be added. The doctrine that
words should not be used to convey ideas
foreign to their real meaning, ought never to be
so perverted as to interfere with their employment in a secondary, derivative or figurative
sense, the legitimate out-growth of their primary
significance. A single illustration will make
this clear. The verb to *endorse* means to put on
the back of; and the United States post-office
department took a mallet for a hammer with
a vengeance when it informed the senders of
registered letters, by a placard formerly displayed in many post-offices, that such letters
" require the name of the sender to be endorsed

on the face of the envelope!"[1]   Endorsed on
the face!   The writer of this notice — who
doubtless imagined that *endorsed* was merely
a more elegant synonym for *written* — might
as well speak of hoisting a load down.   But no
small quantity of what I venture to think rather
wooden-headed criticism has been expended on
the use of the same verb to signify *approve* or
sanction, as in the common expression, to endorse
a candidate or a movement.   It seems to be forgotten that in the usual application of the term
— the endorsing of a note or a check — we have
always in mind, not only the fact that something
is actually written on the back of the paper
in question, but also and chiefly the far more
important fact that the writer of the endorse-
ment, in putting down his name, agrees to
warrant and defend the holder of the document
against loss resulting from his confidence in it.
In other words, he may be said to *back up* the
original maker. ·And just as it is indisputably
good English to speak of a man's friends as

---

[1] It was in consequence of representations by the author
of this paper that the post-office department corrected the
absurdity referred to.

backing him, so is it absolutely good English
to speak of a lawyer endorsing a layman's
opinion about a legal question, or a scholar
endorsing the positions maintained in a book
on classical subjects. To object to such use of
language as this, is to push grammatical criticism to an extreme that is likely only to render
it ridiculous, though if the critics could persuade
the people to follow them, it would result in a
senseless limitation of our choice of words — a
real and by no means inconsiderable injury to
the language.

DEGRADED WORDS.

Note, I beseech you, the many words which men have dragged downward with themselves, and made more or less partakers of their own fall. Having once an honorable significance, they have yet with the deterioration and degeneration of those that used them, or of those about whom they were used, deteriorated and degenerated too. How many, harmless once, have assumed a harmful as their secondary meaning! How many worthy have acquired an unworthy! — *Archbishop Trench.*

IT is a fundamental principle in philology, perhaps *the* fundamental principle, that the words of a living language are constantly changing in their significance, or at least in the precise sense in which by common consent their originally recognized significance is generally taken. Particularly is this true of our comprehensive, flexible, elastic mother tongue, of which the manifold and widely diverse sources of derivation are hardly more varied than the directions in which it is apparently susceptible of ready modification and almost self-impelled development. The process of alteration in the materials of our every-day speech, however, like the action of the geologic forces by which the crust of the earth on which we tread is in our own time undergoing not less real though perhaps less rapid transformation than during the earlier ages, is at once so gradual, and seemingly so natural and inevitable, that we hardly take note of its occurrence; and in the one case as in the other, it might not be difficult, in the absence of information to the contrary, to imagine that all the important changes were made long, long ago, and that the condition of affairs with which we happen to be familiar had been for a considerable period definitely established, and is likely to descend, about as we find it and leave it, to remote posterity. Yet one cannot devote the slightest attention to the subject without perceiving that the truth is quite otherwise — that as the torrents are constantly furrowing and gradually reducing the mountains, and as the great rivers are ever pushing out their deltas into the sea, so

3

are the necessities, and the practices, necessary or not, of our civilized life, every day
extending, diminishing, or in some way modi-
fying, the scope and import of the words we
use. Some familiar terms are parting company by degrees with their literal meaning,
retaining only their derivative sense, like the
verb *transpire*, now very rarely used of material things, but defined by Johnson a century
ago as meaning, first, "to be emitted by
insensible vapor," and only secondarily "to
escape from secrecy to notice," with the
remark that the latter sense is "lately inno-
vated from France, without necessity."[1] Other
words, formerly very general in their significance, have become limited by custom to
a particular subdivision of the large class of
objects they once denoted, like the noun
cattle, which not long ago included all beasts

[1] Judging of the future by the past, it would not be surprising — though much to be regretted — if the still more
recent use of *transpire* as synonymous with *occur*, which has
already effected its entrance into the dictionaries (not into
the language of careful speakers), should come in time, not
only to full equality with the present meaning, but even to
supersede it.

of pasture but is at present, in this country
at least, commonly restricted within the limits
of a single genus. Another group, moving
in precisely the opposite direction, have within
recent times superadded a new quality to
the meaning they formerly embraced, such
for instance as the word *admiration*, which
now means wonder combined with strong
approval, but is used by the translators of
the Bible, in Revelation xvii. 6, for wonder
decidedly without approval, St. John being
made to tell us that he looked "with great
admiration" upon the woman drunken with
the blood of saints and martyrs. Others
again, and no small number, have gradually
made their way upward in the scale of respectability, ridding themselves by degrees
of the shade of evil association that once
rendered them objectionable — such for instance as *fun*, which the old lexicographers
brand as a "low, cant word," indicative of
something quite different from the innocent
merriment for which we now regard it as a
synonym. Others finally, like the verb *to
let*, having formerly represented two different

roots of entirely different meanings, have
gone utterly out of use as regards one of
them, retaining perhaps the signification that
was originally the less familiar of the two.

But in this tossing ocean of a language,
where the constituent waves are ever rising
and falling, advancing and receding, altering
their relative positions, and changing in their
forms and aspects, there is plainly to be dis-
cerned, nevertheless, the existence of certain
well marked currents; and it is one of these
currents that it is the purpose of this chapter
inadequately and for brief distance to endeavor to trace — namely, the group of changes
which keep a record of the follies, weaknesses
and common faults of humankind, and the
daily trials and disappointments that flow
from them; the alterations in the meanings
of words which are plainly due to the unwise
or culpable practices of those who use them.
Many of the facts referred to for illustration
are of course familiar — so familiar indeed
that it is rarely possible to give credit to the
authors who originally noted them.

I.

To take as the first instance a case where the change is still in progress, there is the adjective *pitiful*, which at present we almost invariably employ in an evil sense. "A pitiful subterfuge," we say; that is, a transparent and contemptible attempt at fraud. Yet the dictionaries with one accord give the good meanings precedence, — either "melancholy, moving compassion, deserving to be pitied" (exemplified in the watchman's ejaculation, "pitiful sight!" on discovering the dead body of Juliet), or else "full of pity, tender," as in the three instances in which only the word occurs in King James' Bible. It needs no conjecture to discover the reason and method of this gradual drifting in meaning from good to bad. Whoever has heard a "pitiful" story of his woes from a wandering solicitor of charity, and, moved with compassion, has looked into the case only to find an impudent attempt at deceit, has the explanation before him in characters which he

may run that readeth. The "pitiful" story
becomes provocative of scorn and indigna-
tion; and the ignominy of the transaction
attaches itself to the word that described its
first appearance, dragging down with it the
innocent adjective, and fitting it for compan-
ionship with actions and conditions diametri-
cally opposite to those with which it originally
found place.

If misery loves company, there is no lack of
consolation for *pitiful*, in this unfortunate rele-
gation to infamous uses. At least four other
adjectives have travelled far in the same direction and by much the same route — *apparent*,
ostensible, *plausible* and *specious*. The first of
these commonly (not always, the transformation as yet being incomplete, but commonly)
carries with it in these days at least an insinuation that the thing to which it is applied is
not really quite what it seems — that we must
not be surprised in fact if the truth of the
matter turns out to be very different from its
apparent condition. This insinuation is, so to
speak, a fungus of comparatively recent growth
upon the real meaning of the word, gradually

fostered beyond doubt by a series of painful discoveries. Bailey's whole definition of *apparent*, in 1764, was "that plainly appears, certain, evident, manifest, plain, visible." Thus we still say an "heir apparent," meaning an heir beyond question or dispute, but as far as common usage is concerned, we should hardly employ a word like *certain* as a synonym of *apparent*, the present practice being rather to consider the two adjectives as almost contradictory of each other. Closely similar is the history of *ostensible*, which was formerly understood in its etymological meaning, "capable of being shown," but now conveys, as the Encyclopædic dictionary says, "the idea of sham or pretence." As regards *plausible* and *specious*, they are manifestly only the English forms of the Latin *plausibilis* and *speciosus*,[1] of which the first indicated primarily the possession of qualities deserving of applause, as "*plausibilis nomen*" in Cicero; while *speciosus* is commonly

---

[1] These words, like many others of classical derivation, came into English, not directly, but through living European languages, chiefly the French ; but that fact is of no consequence for the present purpose, so long as they have preserved enough of their original form to be recognized as the same.

best rendered by such expressions as "having a good shape, beautiful, handsome, fine or splendid." What a commentary it is upon the proverbial deceitfulness of appearances in this uncertain world, that these terms, which really indicate that a thing seems to be all right, have come to convey so sharply the implication that it is all wrong!

There is a noun too that started earliest of all in the same *descensus Averni*, and has long since reached a point so low that its hereditary claim to respectability has been almost forgotten. This is *hypocrite*, the Greek Ὑποκριτής in a modern dress — and Ὑποκριτής, as everybody knows, meant originally nothing but a player or actor. Roscius, the elegant speaker and beloved instructor of the greatest Roman orator, was by virtue of his art a *hypocrite*. Plainly the first step downward was taken when the word began to be used figuratively — when men were called hypocrites (in English or Greek) because their life was found to resemble the histrionic art in striving to appear to be different from what it was. It cannot have taken the common-sense of mankind long time

to perceive that such dissimulation is almost
always for evil purposes — the sheep's raiment
covering the ravening wolf. And so it has
come to pass that when we wish to indicate
the assumption of virtue for the intents of vice,
the word that springs most readily to the lips
is the once well-thought-of " hypocrite."

To *counterfeit*, likewise, was formerly only
to imitate, conveying no insinuation as at
present that the imitation was designed to be
fraudulently substituted for the original — this
added insinuation having been developed by
the same process as the present evil significance of the word hypocrite. To *equivocate*
was merely to call two things by the same
name, not necessarily to mean one while leading the hearer to understand the other. *Tinsel*
was really woven of the precious metals, or
supposed to be, until the detection of oft-
repeated frauds caused it to be taken for
granted that the appearance of exceptional
richness and value in ornamental trappings of
this material is nothing but the appearance,
without reality.

Finally under this head should be mentioned

the group of words most characteristic in their present meaning of the special vice of deliberate attempt at deception — the verb *pretend* and its derivatives. To say nothing of the innocent meaning indicated by their Latin origin, it is not so very long since they were used in English without any evil implication. Ash, 1775, mentions among his definitions of the verb, " to claim, to demand as right," and gives " a claim" as the first equivalent of the noun pretension. Johnson informs us that a pretender is " one who lays claim to anything " — that, and nothing more. A claimant, whether justly or unjustly, was in his view a *pretender*, and the butcher Orton, had he lived in England a century earlier, might have been spoken of as " pretending to be Sir Roger Tichborne " without the slightest intimation on the part of the speaker that the story was not believed. In the third part of King Henry Sixth, published 1623, Shakspeare makes Sir John Montgomery demand of King Edward at the gates of York, " why shall we fight, if you *pretend* no title? " and in the same breath, " if you'll not here proclaim yourself our king, I'll leave you

to your fortune "— using *pretend* almost inter-
changeably with *proclaim*. Milton indeed, forty
years later, wrote, "this let him know, lest,
wilfully transgressing, he *pretend* surprisal"
(*Paradise Lost*, v, 244), and elsewhere uses the
word in the same manner; but the innocent
meaning has lingered in literature for nearly
two centuries longer. As historically applied
for instance to the son and grandson of James
II. of England, it can hardly have been originally intended to signify much more than
claimant; for the unfortunate princes made no
attempt at representing themselves to be anything but what they were, though they unquestionably *laid claim* to a kingly dignity that
the nation was not anxious to concede to them.
In the denoument of Lord Lytton's masterpiece,
" My Novel," to take an instance within our
own times, it may be remembered that Peschiera,
in his scathing exposure of the villainy of
Randal Leslie, speaks of him as " pretending "
to the hand of Violante; and though there was
certainly no love lost between the two worthies
at that juncture, yet the context makes it clearly
evident that this particular word is intended in

no reproachful sense — the dashing count meant
only to represent the minor scoundrel as his
rival, seeking what he himself sought, and by
much the same means, and *pretend* in his
mouth is the exact equivalent of *aspire.* Yet
who does not feel, now-a-days, the more than
suggestion of a charge of fraud that is conveyed
when we speak of any one as " pretending," or
as being a " pretender " ? — and indeed Webster,
reversing the earlier order of definitions, renders
the noun as meaning, first, " one who simulates
or feigns," and only secondarily, " one who lays
claim," in which he doubtless interprets correctly our modern usage. What deduction can
we draw from such a progression in meaning
toward the bad but this — that it has been the
common experience that people are apt to claim
more than their due?

There is yet one more word that may perhaps be considered as allied to the foregoing, if
the history of its changing sense, as given by
Barclay — an author of no great fame, who
nevertheless managed to gather a good deal of
curious and interesting matter — is true. This
is *legend,* of which he says, writing about ninety

years ago, that it was originally " a book in the church containing the lessons that were to be read in divine service; from hence the word was applied to the histories of the lives of the saints, because chapters were read out of them at matins, but as the 'golden legend,' compiled by James de Varase about the year 1290, contained several ridiculous and romantic stories, the word is now used to signify any incredible or unauthentic narrative." That is to say, legends, books highly esteemed, have been so often found to contain glaring falsehoods — for it can hardly be that the change is wholly attributable to the single instance mentioned by our author — that the very word which used to denote only that the composition to which it was applied ought to be read, now serves rather to warn the reader that it ought not to be believed !

II.

ANOTHER common fault with our not-too-truthful humanity, nearly allied to the practice of exaggerating one's own deserts and concealing blemishes, is that of unduly depreciating the

merits of other people, and particularly of despising beyond reason such classes of the community as we think below us; and this habit, as
might be anticipated, has made its mark upon
our language.   There are a number of words
that formerly indicated little more than inferior
social or political position, but which have come
to embody the charge of something much worse.
Thus a *villain* was at first, as Trench puts it,
only a serf or bondsman " (*villanus*), because
attached to the *villa* or farm; " and secondly
" the peasant who, it is taken for granted," [and
this is the root of the matter] " will be churlish,
selfish, dishonest, and of evil moral conditions,
these having come to be assumed as always be-
longing to him, and to be permanently associ-
ated with his name, by those higher classes of
society who in the main commanded the springs
of language.   At the third step, nothing of the
meaning which the etymology suggests, nothing of *villa*, survives any longer; the peasant is
quite dismissed, and the evil moral conditions of
him who is called by this name alone remain."
Thus Barrow rather superciliously remarks that
foul language " is termed villainy, as being

proper for rustic boors, who, having their minds debased by being conversant in meanest affairs, do vent their sorry passions in such strains."

The term *boor*, just quoted, was likewise originally descriptive of nothing worse than "a husbandman," "a plowman," "a country fellow," and the word or its Hollandish representative is still applied, without offence, to the wealthy and presumably well mannered Dutch planters of South Africa. A *churl* was a free tenant at will, or, as some trace the derivation, only a person of remarkable physical prowess. A *kern* was a footman or foot-soldier of rural extraction. A *pagan* (to quote Trench again) was "first a villager, then a heathen villager, lastly a heathen." *Heathen* itself meant originally only a dweller on the heath or open country. *Incivility* was merely the customary behavior, in the eyes of city residents, of their somewhat unpolished acquaintances from the interior; and the epithet *savage* indicated for a long time nothing more than relationship to the forest, or at worst a wild or uncultivated state, without the implication of anything like ferocity. This must have been Milton's conception when he wrote of

a "savage hill," and a "savage wilderness;"
and Dryden's too, who speaks of "savage ber-
ries of the wood."

Not only, however, are dwellers in towns addicted to under-estimating their brethren of the
fields, but the smaller minds of every country
are apt to consider their land the flowery kingdom, and to despise unreasonably the outside
nations. The prevalence of this folly is well
illustrated by the present degradation of the
adjective *outlandish*, which ought of course to
mean only foreign, as it plainly did in the seventeenth century, when Translator-General Hol-
land, rendering Pliny into English, made him
refer to "outlandish wheat." The *uncouth*,
also, was once merely the unknown or unfamiliar; a *vagabond* or a *harlot* was a wanderer or
stranger, not necessarily of disreputable character; and a *barbarian*, in Greek, was a man of
different nationality from the speaker.

Idiot meant originally in English, as in its
native tongue, only a private person, or at worst
an unlearned man, these two constituting the
whole definition given by Bailey, except when
used as a technical term in law. Jeremy Tay-

lor, in the middle of the seventeenth century, remarked that " humility is a duty in great ones as well as in idiots; " and Blount, a contemporary of the good bishop, says: " Christ was received of idiots, while he was rejected and persecuted by the priests, doctors and rabbis." From this meaning, however, the word speedily descended to the level of the lowest classes in society; then came to indicate dense and stupid ignorance, and finally attached itself to persons absolutely void of understanding, natural fools, innocents or simpletons, as Webster has it. One can imagine the effect, in these days, of a minister's addressing his congregation as composed in part of idiots !

The appellation *caitiff*, which implies at present, and has done so for a long time, the possession of certain highly uncommendable traits of character, is traced by Johnson to the Italian *cattivo*, a slave, " whence," says the doctor, " it came to signify a bad man, with some implication of meanness," and he adds: " A slave and a scoundrel are signified by the same words in many languages."

The adjective *vulgar*, again, was once almost

4

synonymous with such innocent terms as general, public, and even national.   A *mob* was not
much more than the common people, the crowd,
having only in recent times come to imply,
adopting Worcester's expression, " a crowd excited to some violent or unlawful act," the select
few always recklessly imputing evil purposes
to the many who they think should rank below them. *Base, mean* and *lewd* were terms
applied of old to the mass of the population,
as distinguished from the gentry or clergy, and
indicated nothing worse than this.   Spenser
writes, in the *Faerie Queene :*

> " But virtuous women wisely understand
>   That they were born to base humility,
>   Unless the Heavens them lift to lawful sovereignty."

In one of Latimer's sermons, we read: " It
might please the king to accept into his favor
a mean man, of simple degree and birth, not
born to any possessions."   As for *lewd*, it seems
to be only a variation of *lay*, a lewd fellow being
etymologically merely a layman.   So Chaucer,
in the *Canterbury Tales :*

> " For if a priest be foul, on whom we trust,
>   No wonder is a lewid man to rust."

But the rich and the learned have been tempted
so often to despise and slander the poor
and the ignorant, these adjectives have been
coupled so commonly with injurious aspersions,
that we now insult a man, however humble his
station in life, if we call him base, mean or
lewd.

A process of degradation, not dissimilar
from the foregoing in its operation, has been
effected within comparatively recent times also
on the noun *beast* and its derivatives, it seeming to have been found impossible for rational
man to speak of his less highly endowed fellow
creatures without some tinge of scorn gradually attaching itself to the name by which
he calls them. The " beasts " of the Apocalypse are plainly only living beings different
from men; and in Wiclif's version of First Corinthians, five hundred years ago, we find: " It
is sown a beastly body; it shall rise a spiritual
body."

The term *knave*, like the German *knabe*,
meant at first only a boy, well or ill behaved.
In Wiclif's Apocalypse, the woman clothed
with the sun is represented as giving birth

to "a knave child;" and when Shakspeare
wrote "good knave" (in Twelfth Night), and
"gentle knave" (in Julius Cæsar), there was
nothing incongruous in the expressions. Next
it indicated a servant; there is said to be an
early version of the New Testament in which
the Apostle Paul is styled "the knave of Jesus
Christ;" and it is doubtless in the sense of a
serving man or attendant to the king and queen
that the name was given to the card at whist.
Indeed the knave is called "*le valet*" in French
to this day, — *valet*, by the way, being only
the modern form of the old Gallic *varlet*, our
English varlet.   The words caitiff, knave and
varlet came, however to designate not only a
servant but a cowardly or roguish servant, and
in process of time the original signification has
been quite lost sight of, nothing remaining of
the poor despised dependents but the evil odor
of their supposed bad morals.

A *blackguard*, moreover, was merely a scul-
lion, — that is, *the* "black guard" was the
company of such servitors, who accompanied
persons of quality on their journeys, to take
care of the pots and kettles; and the ancient

acceptation of the term involved no necessary conception of ruffianly manners.

A *menial* was one of the household or mesnee; *minion* was only a favorite, the French *mignon*. A *brat* was simply a child, however lovely; and an *imp* was a young person, a minor, particularly, it would seem, a young heir. To *imp* is to engraft, and the imps of a family were what we now, adopting precisely the same figure, call the scions. Tusser writes, in "Good Husbandry," 1557:

> "Take heed how thou layest the bane for the rats,
> For poisoning thy servant, thyself, and thy brats."

It is stated that one of the earls of Warwick, who died in boyhood, is commemorated in a mortuary inscription in the chancel of the parish church as "the noble imp;" and Bacon, in his "Pathway unto Prayer," exhorts his readers to "pray for the preservation of the king's most excellent majesty, and for the prosperous success of his entirely beloved son, Edward our Prince, that most angelic imp."

Now it may be, of course, that a part of the new turpitude which has gradually attached itself to all these words — villain, boor, churl, kern, pagan, savage, vagabond, harlot, barbarian, idiot, caitiff, vulgar, mob, base, mean, lewd, beastly, blackguard, minion, brat, imp, and others like them — is attributable to the actual discovery of unexpected vices in the classes to whom they primarily referred; but it seems more probable that the terms have become odious chiefly because of their constant application to those unfortunates whom their betters have thought it proper to regard with some measure of systematic contempt. In either case, the changes in meaning that the whole group have undergone, constitute certainly a very striking instance of the power of degradation which man's bad habits are constantly exerting upon the structure of the language that he uses.

III.

BUT it must not be supposed, nevertheless, that all the despising, all the calling of hard names, is to be attributed to the upper ten. A moment's reflection will discover that the

children, the learners, and inferiors of various
grades, have been active, on their part, in bringing about a similar humiliation for the words by
which they designate both the persons and the
opinions of their rulers and instructors.   Here
however, as in the preceding case, there has no
doubt been fault on both sides.   Had the
teachers of youth never assumed a degree of
knowledge beyond their actual attainments, the
words *pedant* and *pedagogue*, both perfectly innocent in their etymology and once inoffensive
in their use, might never have come to convey
the implication of owlish self-conceit.   Had
the schoolmen of the middle ages devoted a
larger share of their attention to the acquisition
of really useful and practical knowledge, and
exercised their wits less exclusively with " subtill
quiddities," the name of their great exem-
plar, Duns Scotus, might never have been corrupted, in form and meaning, into our modern
dunce.   Had the expounders of scientific discovery, and the preachers of religion, been invariably careful to confine their inculcations within
the limits of certain truth, and to allow to their
disciples the exercise of untrammeled reason in

weighing the doctrines they were expected to
accept, the term *theory*, which ought to denote
a reasonable opinion logically deduced from
a sufficient number of established facts, might
never have sunk so near to becoming a synonym of the wildest guessing; and *dogma*, which
properly indicates only a tenet or principle of
belief, might never have carried with it the im-
putation of obstinate and unwarranted assertion.
Had students really in possession of superior
knowledge employed it more generally for the
benefit of their fellow-men, rather than to bewil-
der and delude them, the term *wizard* (a wise
man) might never have descended to equiva-
lency with charlatan and impostor.

Had absolute rulers, again, exerted their authority mainly for the good of their subjects,
the appellations *tyrant* and *despot* might still
have been free from more than shade of censure
that now clings to them. *Tyrant*, indeed, began
very early to imply reproach, and in Latin is
commonly used in the same unfavorable sense
as in English, but in Greek we find it applied to
the mild Pisistratus. *Despot*, it will be remembered, was frequently employed in antiquity as

a respectful form of address in approaching a
monarch. Thus in Herodotus' account of the
debate in the Persian cabinet over the invasion
of Greece, the statesman Mardonius, beginning
the speech that "smoothed over" the opinion
of Xerxes, calls him "Ὦ δέσποτα" — rather inadequately rendered by Cary, "sir."   And in
much later times, if the tradition preserved by
Döllinger in his " Myths of the Middle Ages " is
to be believed, the announcement, "Ἄρρην ἡμῖν
ἐστὶν ὁ δεσπότης," constituted an essential for-
mality in the enthronement of the popes. In no
such case as this, can the Greek progenitor of
our English *despot* be supposed to convey any
uncomplimentary notion. The modern conception of selfish and cruel oppression that is now
so firmly united with the definition of either of
these words, is doubtless the outgrowth at once
of the bad use of unlimited authority on the
part of the average ruler, and of the proneness
of the average subject to cast what opprobrium
he can and dares upon the powers that be.

IV.

TURNING now to words relating to the passions and appetites, we shall find several whose
altered meanings tell plainly the story of repeated indulgence in wrong directions, or at
least of grovelling tastes. The degradation of
the word *paramour*, formerly used by Spenser
and others in a perfectly innocent sense, and
the vulgar misuse sometimes to be noticed of
the beautiful word *love*, which ought to express
one's feelings toward his child, his wife, his
mother, or his God — the misuse of this word
by connecting it with the names of things
we eat — are cases in point. To *carouse*, again,
was once only to drink, with however great
a degree of decorum and propriety. "The
queen carouses to thy fortune, Hamlet," so pro-
claims that august lady in the last scene of the
tragedy, referring plainly to the taking of a
single glass, by way of formal compliment. But
as our affections are so apt to be set upon things
that perish with the using, and as the enjoyment
of intoxicants has been found so often to degen-

erate into their lawless and injurious abuse, we
have come by degrees to conceive the incongruous notion of " loving " a favorite eatable,
and our designation of the slightest possible
use of wine has grown so swollen and distorted,
like the persons of the depraved beings whose
bad habits have brought about the change, as to
imply the highest degree of riotous excess.

The selfish and malevolent passions, too, have
been at work upon our vocabulary.   Charles
Francis Adams, some years ago, took occasion
to characterize the British nation as greatly
"*addicted* to commerce," for which expression
he was censured by sundry newspapers, on the
ground that commerce is not a vice.   Truly it
is not; but why should we never speak of persons or peoples as *addicted* (or *prone*, or *apt*,
which are other expressions of exactly the same
kind) to do anything but what is evil? — the
words having equally proper application, both
by etymology and by the authority of ancient
usage, to good practices and to bad.   Why, indeed, had not common experience persistently
given its testimony in support of something
very like the much abused theological doctrine

of total depravity, the doctrine that "we are utterly indisposed to all good, and wholly inclined to all evil"?

Indolence, again, once signified merely a condition of freedom from pain or excitement, and it would seem that its present parity with laziness must be due to the fact that humankind is not likely greatly to exert itself unless stimulated by the actual presence or the apprehended peril of some sort of discomfort. To be *careless*, in Pope's time, was to be free from anxiety — not culpably negligent, as now. "Thus wisely careless, innocently gay," he writes. In present common language, we seldom consider carelessness wise. *Indifference* was impartiality, so that it was once a compliment to say of a magistrate that he administered justice indifferently, though we should now infer from the remark that his decisions were thoughtless and as likely to be wrong as right.

To *covet* means, of course, properly speaking, only to desire eagerly, the French *convoiter*, and the expression was formerly employed, as by the translators of the Bible in First Corinthians (xii. 31), "covet earnestly the best things " — without that implication of evil which man's bad habit, his proneness to covet more particularly what he knows he ought not to have, has fastened upon it.

The expression " to *inflame*," which we seldom hear now-a-days except in connection with some evil feeling, was used of old in reference to the good passions quite as freely as the bad, examples of which practice can be found in many hymns still sung. "To *denounce*," also, "to *instigate*," "to *conspire*," "to *abet*," and "to *provoke*," are verbs that we hardly ever employ at the present day except in reference to wrong doing, though just as correctly applicable to endeavors in the most praiseworthy directions, and once so used. An *accomplice* was not formerly by implication the assistant in an *evil* undertaking, as at present — see I. Henry VI, v. 2: "Success unto our valiant general, and happiness to his accomplices!" *Animosity*, in Sir Thomas Browne's "Urn Burial," 1658, meant courage, as where he tells us that Cato confirmed "his wavering hand to animosity" by reading the Greek philosophers. To *wrangle* was formerly simply to argue, however politely

— an ancient usage of which we still hear an echo in the honorary appointment of "wranglers" at Cambridge University — though, as need hardly be said, a *wrangle* is now a noisy altercation, generally rather assertive than argumentative. So "to *have words*" with a man is now in most cases to quarrel with him, so great is the tendency of animated discussions, those in which we notice chiefly the great flow of words on both sides, to degenerate into heated disputes.

But perhaps the most striking instance of the spoiling of words of this class is that which is furnished by the verbs *retaliate, resent,* and their derivatives. The writer was once present at the parting of that scholarly but somewhat eccentric divine, the Rev. Dr. Samuel Hanson Cox, from a gentleman to whom he was indebted for hospitality, and to whom he said: "You may be certain, sir, that I shall be glad of any opportunity to display my resentment of your attentions." The host looked rather blank, as well he might, and the doctor explained: "That word resentment, sir, is a good word that has been brought into disgrace by man's wickedness. It

only indicates a feeling-back, a desire to recip-
rocate, and was once employed as well in relation to benefits as to injuries. But we have so
short a memory for kindness, and so vague an
intention of returning it, while our perceptions
of wrong done us are so acute, and our inclina-
tions toward revengeful purposes so strong, that
one is actually not understood in these days if
he speaks of resenting anything but an affront
or an attack!" This position is unquestionably
sound; and almost the same remarks apply also
to the companion words *retaliation* and *retaliate*,
which certainly no one would think of employ-
ing now except in connection with some kind of
injury. Yet to retaliate is only to pay back,
whether good or evil, as to resent is to feel back,
whether with gratitude or with anger; and examples of the use of both words in the good
sense abound in our earlier literature, particularly in the sermons of the seventeenth century,
with whose authors they seem to have been
favorite terms. Thus Isaac Barrow strongly
enjoins the duty of cultivating "resentment of
our obligations to God," and in another passage
remarks that "honor renders a man a faithful

resenter of courtesies;" and Edmund Calamy
says: "God takes what is done to others as
done to himself, and by promise obliges himself
to full retaliation." Dryden, too, writing at
about the same period, has the statement: "The
king expects a return from them, that the kindness which he has shown them may be retaliated
on those of his own persuasion." Such expressions grate harshly on modern ears, but that
is because the words have become soiled and
polluted by the unworthy purposes to which
they have now so long been generally restricted.
And the language, let it be noticed, is just so
much the poorer in consequence, for we have no
exact synonyms with which, for their former
and better use, we may replace them.

V.

ANOTHER unfortunate trait of character whose
prevalence is curiously illustrated in a similar
way, is that suggested by the adjectives *meddle-
some* and *officious*. To meddle with anything
was once merely to concern one's self with it, no
implication of any impertinence or other impro-

priety being conveyed. *Officious*, in Bailey's time, had preserved exactly the meaning of its Latin ancestor, " ready to do one a good office, serviceable, very obliging," and it is in this sense that Titus Andronicus uses it when he says [v. 2]: " Come, come, be every one officious to make this banquet." *Pragmatical* and *busybody* also, though perhaps always involving some degree of censure in their English use, *ought* certainly by every principle of etymology to be susceptible of an innocent if not a laudatory application. Πραγματικός means " active, able, business-like or prudent." A busybody is plainly a person who is busy; and why, in either case, should it always be taken for granted that the individual of whom these terms are predicated is active about business that he might better let alone, unless the common experience of those who have employed the words has taught them that people are for the most part rather more likely to exert themselves in the pursuit of uncommendable enterprises than in the practice of their appropriate occupations?

5

VI.

OUR evil tendency to grumble and complain of our surroundings, and to find fault with our fellow-men, has likewise been instrumental in the degradation of a number of common expressions. Can it be believed, for instance, that *homely* would ever have come to mean ugly among people cultivating a due spirit of contentment with their daily lot? The adjectives *chronic* and *inveterate*, also, and the nouns *plight* and *predicament*, ought to be as freely applicable to desirable states and conditions as to the reverse. Dr. Cuyler once wrote, in the *Evangelist* : "We pastors set great store by chronic Christians; " but in present common usage it cannot be denied that these terms are seldom heard except in relation to things evil. A *catastrophe*, too, is really only the final act of a drama, whether tragic or comic, and has perhaps become so nearly the synonym of *disaster* chiefly because we are so apt to take it for granted, in our talk, if not in our real convictions, that things generally turn out badly. The same feeling is shown in our constant restriction of the use of the adjective *ominous* and the verbs to *bode* and to *presage*, which words we never use except in connection with misfortunes. Etymologically, appearances might be *ominous* of joy, or *presage* great success; we might have *forebodings* of the most roseate hue as well as of the gloomiest.

To *censure* was once merely to express an opinion, as in Richard III.: "Will you go and give your censures in this business?" To *traduce* was simply to blame, not to slander; so Enobarbus speaks of Antony (Antony and Cleopatra, iii. 7) as being "*traduced* for levity." But our judgment of each other is so often uncharitably and undeservedly severe that the meanings of these words have become limited to unfavorable judgment and unfounded condemnation; and it appears to me that *animadvert* and *criticise* are going the same way as *censure*; we apply them much more frequently, I think, to the expression of blame than of commendation.[1]

The *epithet egregious* might formerly have

1 See Atlantic Monthly, vol. 53, p. 578, April, 1884.

been coupled with the name of the most distinguished philosopher, poet or statesman;
but we are so much readier at abusing our
neighbors than praising them, that the term
epithet has dropped almost entirely its good
use; and we are so likely, in characterizing
any person as at all peculiar, which is all that
egregious really signifies, to mean that he is
peculiarly disagreeable, that one rather expects
now-a-days some highly damaging appellation
to follow, when a man is mentioned as " an
egregious — " and there the speaker pauses.
So with *arrant*, formerly the same as *errant*,
and meaning merely *wandering*, but later used
as synonymous with *notorious*, and since 1575
(according to Dr. J. A. H. Murray) "as an
opprobrious intensive."

VII.

MAN'S propensity to over-reach his fellows
when he can, and to take unfair advantage of
their necessities, has branded several words
with new opprobrium. To *prevent* is really
only to get ahead of, or to precede, as in the

English Common Prayer: "Let thy grace always prevent and follow us;" and Hamlet (ii. 2), "So shall my anticipation prevent your discovery." But alas! those who reach first a desirable goal are so wont to take advantage of their position, not to help others get there too, but to block the way if possible, that the verb which ought only to describe the arrival of the first-comers in advance of the rest, is now understood as implying also their doing the best they can to monopolize the good fortune, and *prevent* others from sharing it.

Another illustration of the same principle, still stronger perhaps, is furnished by the word *rival*. Rivals were at first only the occupiers of the banks of the same stream, and a little later, partners or co-laborers in the same enterprise. It is in this sense that Bernardo speaks of Horatio and Marcellus as the rivals of his watch. But it came to be perceived that joint owners and partners are very apt to quarrel, each doing his best to possess himself of all the advantages of the combination, until at last the word, in our present usage, has come to involve the entirely modern addi-

tion of a conflict of interest, and more or less
hard-feeling between the parties.

Artful, so late as the time of Johnson, meant
only skillful, not tricky. *Usury* was once merely
interest money, however moderate the amount
and however legal and equitable the charge.
A *cheat*, or escheatour, was a royal officer in
England who attended to the sequestration of
estates that were forfeited to the crown, and
the corrupt practices of these men led it to be
commonly believed that to "cheat" a man was
to deprive him of his property *unfairly* —
which meaning is now the only one recognized.
To *embezzle* was to spend rashly and foolishly,
but it was applied for a long time to the man's
own property — " Mr. Hackluit died, leaving
a fair estate to an unthrift son, who embezzled
it " [1] — that is, wasted it — until it was discovered that spendthrifts are apt to become
thieves as well. A *defalcation* was formerly
only a diminution or abatement, as in Burke:
"The natural method in reformation would be
to take the estimates and show what may be
safely defalcated from them." Its present use,

[1] Thomas Fuller, " *Worthies of England*," 1662.

as implying knavery in the diminution, is possibly due in part to some supposed connection with "default" and "defaulter," to which words it is by etymology only very distantly if at all related.

VIII.

OF the great multitude of other degraded words that do not so readily fall into classes, but illustrate nevertheless each one the prevalence of some blameworthy course of action or thought, may be instanced *gossip*, which denoted first a fellow sponsor in baptism, next an intimate friend, and finally a too-talkative and therefore often dangerous companion; *voluble*, which was only fluent (and not unduly fluent as at present) when Bishop Hacket, a little more than two hundred years ago, wrote of Archbishop Abbott that " he was of a grave and voluble eloquence;" *conceit*, properly the equivalent of *idea* or *opinion*, but rarely used now except for such opinions as the speaker deems ill-founded or absurd; *profane*, which originally meant only secular or non-sacred, as we still say " profane history," and its opposite, *fanatic*, which really signifies about the same as *inspired;*

libertine and *miscreant*, formerly synonymous
with free-thinker and infidel, and having reference solely to the man's opinions instead of
his actions; *obsequious*, which originally implied merely the exercise of affectionate and
becoming obedience; *fussy*, which was once the
same as *busy;* an *apology*, which was of old
only a defence, by no means implying that the
thing apologized for was in the slightest degree
admitted to be improper, but merely that it had
been attacked; *ringleader* and *notorious*, which
have only in modern times become restricted to
their present evil sense; *bush-whacking*, which
was originally "a harmless word, denoting simply the process of propelling a boat by pulling
the bushes, or of beating them down in order
to open a way through a thicket;"[1] a *proser*,
which term really indicates only a person who
writes prose, whether tiresome or the reverse;
casuistry, the science of determining what is
duty, but more generally applied to specious
attempts at making the worse appear the better
reason; *emissary*, a messenger, but almost
always now a messenger of evil purposes;

[1] Schele de Vere, " Americanisms," p. 89.

demagogue, a leader of the people — Dean Swift calls Demosthenes and Cicero demagogues, intending to do them honor; *silly*, which was originally synonymous with *harmless* or *innocent; willful*, which should mean not much more than *determined*, though in practice we never hear of the willful performance of anything but evil; *audacious*, now understood to mean *impudent*, but formerly the same as *brave; beldame*, originally a grandmother; *abominable*, which once meant only *excessive* or *monstrous; barefaced*, which for a long time signified *undisguised*, and only more recently, *shameless; rife*, which I think we seldom employ now except in connection with something unpleasant; *virago*, which Johnson defines, first, as "a female warrior," quoting from Peacham — "Melpomene is represented like a virago or manly lady, with a majestic and grave countenance;" the adjective *jesuitical*, and the verb to *jew*, which are invariably used in a highly offensive sense not at all implied by their etymology.

IX.

NOT to prolong, however, this catalogue of human frailties, there is one bad habit that gives constant annoyance in our daily life, and seems sometimes to prepare the way for all the others — the habit of procrastination, unnecessary and vexatious delay when action is demanded. A vice so common could hardly fail to make its impression on the language. Accordingly we find that certain adverbs of time which are and have been very frequently employed in promising immediate attention to duty, have lost by degrees a large share of their former intensity (promises of this kind being so often broken), and have become so weakened and enervated as quite to obscure the sense in many passages of the older writers. Thus Bailey's definition of the word *presently* — which is "at present, at this time, now," as exemplified by Cardinal Beaufort in King Henry Sixth [part two, 1, 1], "this weighty business will not brook delay; I'll to the Duke of Suffolk presently" — this definition is marked

"obsolete" by Webster, though that meaning
still seems to survive in Great Britain, for such
expressions as "Gen. Ramsay is presently
visiting at the castle" are not uncommon in
British papers. Yet the American lexicographer is indisputably correct when he proceeds to mention, as the synonyms of this
adverb in its more common applications, the
words " soon, before long, after a little time " —
which embody quite a different conception.

As regards the similar term *by-and-by*, the
case is if possible still stronger, the ancient
meaning still more debilitated in modern usage.
Of course this word in our present understanding of it, invariably implies considerable delay,
but we need only turn to the Greek Testament
to discover that King James' translators considered it the equivalent for the most em-
phatic adverbs that the original tongue can
furnish to indicate instant and hurried action —
εὐθὺς, εὐθέως and ἐξαυτῆς. These words mean
suddenly, hastily, rashly, at the very point of
time; and are rendered "straightway," "immediately" and " forthwith " in the Bible itself,
when *by-and-by* is not used. In the account

given by Ulysses in the Ajax of his breathless
and frantic pursuit of the mad warrior who had
butchered the flocks and their guardians, Sopho-
cles makes him say: "And to me a watchman that espied him bounding over the plains
alone, with freshly reeking sword, tells it; and
εὐθέως [that is, *instantly*] I hurry close on his
steps." Fancy rendering this, as is done with
the same word in the Bible, "*By-and-by* I hurry
on his steps!" How completely such a translation destroys the coherence of the narrative!
What a flood of light is thrown too upon the
real intent of the sacred writers, when we substitute (as is done in the Revised Version) the
stronger and now more accurate expressions
for the indefinite *by-and-by*, as in Matthew xiii.
21: "Yet hath he not root in himself, for when
tribulation or persecution ariseth because of the
word," not "*by-and-by*," but STRAIGHTWAY "he
is offended," does not hold out at all — makes
no effort for a single moment to breast the current! Again, Mark vi. 25: "And she came
in straightway with haste unto the king, and
asked, saying, I will that thou give me," not
"*by-and-by*," but FORTHWITH, "in a charger,

the head of John the Baptist." Finally, Luke
xxi. 9 : "But when ye shall hear of wars and
commotions, be not terrified, for these things
must first come to pass, but the end is not"—
IMMEDIATELY. And if the gradual fading out
of the original intense emphasis of these words
is largely due, as every consideration seems
to render probable, to the fact that people have
so often said they would do things "presently"
or "by-and-by," and then have neglected them,
so that in process of time the idea of more or
less delay has become thoroughly involved in
the common understanding of the words themselves — what a commentary does it furnish
upon the prevalence of this habit of procrastination, that these terms, once the strongest that
could be found to picture hurried and impatient
action, have come at last, as indisputably in
ordinary usage they have, to denote so vaguely
an indefinite period, at an indefinite distance,
in the indefinite and uncertain future !

THE ENGLISH OF THE REVISED NEW TESTAMENT.

The truth is, — as all who have given real thought to the subject must be aware, — the phenomena of language are among the most subtle and delicate imaginable : the problem of translation, one of the most many-sided and difficult that can be named. And if this holds universally, in how much greater a degree when the book to be translated is the Bible ! . . . Not the least service which the revisionists have rendered has been the proof their work affords, how very seldom our authorized version is materially wrong. . . . It is but fair to add that their work bears marks of an amount of conscientious labor which those only can fully appreciate who have made the same province of study to some extent their own. — *London Quarterly Review.*

IT is to be feared that the revisers of the New Testament, looking back now after the lapse of a dozen years and more since the version of 1881 was issued, can hardly feel that the public appreciation of their efforts has been quite what was expected. No important church has formally approved the revised version; no great Bible society has undertaken to circulate it;

and while the most competent authorities appear
to be pretty nearly unanimous in commending
alike the Greek readings adopted by the revisers in disputed passages, and the fidelity with
which the original is, on the whole, represented
by their rendering, it nevertheless cannot be
denied that so far as the *English* of the book
is concerned, a large part of the criticism which
has appeared — bursting forth in (somewhat
discordant) chorus immediately after the publication of the work, and continuing at intervals
ever since — has been of an unfavorable tone,
and that this judgment operates powerfully in
perpetuating the supremacy of the King James
translation. It cannot be denied, either, that
the impartial reader who takes pains to examine
the matter without prejudice either in favor of
or against alterations *qua* alterations, will find
what really seem to be an unreasonably large
number of verbal blemishes marring the great
work. The following may be mentioned as
instances of rather gross infelicities which should
certainly have been avoided :

1. " Repented himself," whatever it may formerly have been, is surely not good English now.

Yet not only is the archaic phrase retained in
Matt. xxvii. 3; but in Matt. xxi. 29, 32, and
Heb. vii. 21, the modern English of the authorized version is replaced by the utterly obsolete
construction, making *repent* a reflexive verb.

2. In John xix. 29 we now read that "they
put a sponge full of vinegar upon hyssop, and
brought it to his mouth." The authorized version has "put." The verb "bring" indicates
almost invariably, except in the mouths of
the careless or ignorant, a motion *toward the
speaker;* and it is not easy to conjecture by
what possible argument its employment in the
sentence quoted can be regarded as defensible.

3. In 1st Cor. i. 18, we have: "Unto us which
are being saved"; in 2d Cor. ii. 15, "In them
that *are being* saved"; in Col. iii. 10, "The new
man, which *is being* renewed unto knowledge";
and in 2d Tim. iv. 6, "For *I am* already *being*
offered." Much may of course be said — much
has been said — in justification of this construction; but it will be admitted on all sides that
the best practice very seldom employs it.

4. In Matt. v. 35, Heb. i. 13 and x. 13 occur
the cumbrous and cacophonous phrases, "The

footstool of thy feet," "The footstool of his feet," and in 1st Peter iii. 17, "If the will of God should so will." What possible purpose, in an *English* book, is served by these awkward repetitions? And is not the last an absurdity at best, *as we use the words in English?* God can will; and his will can be this or that; but can his will will? The fact that these phrases exactly represent the Greek, is no sufficient reason, surely, for inflicting them on the English reader, the genius and structure of the two languages being so different. Almost as well might the Greek double negative be rendered by two "nots" in one English negative sentence.

5. Not exactly bad English, perhaps, but certainly not good English at the present day, is the old rendering of "single" for ἁπλοῦς in Matt. vi. 22 and Luke xi. 34, which is retained by the revisers. This translation (though of course in a certain sense undeniably accurate) is particularly objectionable, as tending to mislead the reader. We often hear of an "eye single to the public good," meaning an eye turned exclusively in that one direction; and the sense of the passages as we have them in

6

English *appears* to be that if the mind is steadily devoted to one purpose all will be well, which is very different from their real significance.

6. Why is *bits*, in James iii. 3, changed to *bridles ?* Does any one ever think of saying, in ordinary speech, that he puts a " bridle " into a horse's mouth? The poor animal would find his mouth very uncomfortably distended, were such an operation undertaken; and might well apprehend dislocation of the jaws if it were successfully carried out.

7. It is to be regretted that we still read " Simon Bar-Jonah " in Matt. xvi. 17, while in John xxi. 15, 16, 17, it is " Simon, son of John." Of course the " βὰρ " is found in the Greek text in the first case, and not in the others; but the meaning is identical, the Ἰωνᾶ is identical. Why should " he that occupieth the room of the unlearned " be caused to stumble by finding " Bar-Jonah " in one place, and " son of John " elsewhere, while the evangelists intended to write precisely the same thing?

It is not only in single phrases, however, that the revisers made bad work. There are whole classes of words that they handle unskillfully, —

such as the pronouns *thy* and *thine*, *who* and *which* and *that*, which they seem to exchange quite at random; the subjunctive moods of verbs; the adverbs *alway* and *always;* the conjunction *and*, which they use much too freely for the best English practice; and the particles *if, though, whether, unless* and *except*, which they employ rather carelessly and inaccurately. On these points it is hardly needful now to enlarge, for they have been discussed at length in a book called " The Revisers' English," by Mr. G. Washington Moon, a gentleman who had previously done good service in pointing out a number of Dean Alford's errors. This book is worth reading. Mr. Moon always writes entertainingly, on grammatical subjects at least, and generally teaches sound doctrine, though readers are likely to be somewhat prejudiced against his conclusions by his unfortunate manner of stating them, for he is afflicted with so irascible a temper that he can seldom content himself with attacking what he regards as bad practice without at the same time reviling every critic that disagrees with him. He is moreover a little too much tied down to certain hard-and-fast interpretations of general laws to which the best usage recognizes, and always will recognize, and always ought to recognize, a number of seeming — perhaps not real — exceptions.

Of one exemplification of the last-named defect in Mr. Moon's grammatical teaching, illustrations may be found abundantly in his criticisms of the revisers' English, and the matter is worth considering — not, of course, that it is highly important whether Mr. Moon is right or wrong about it, but because he opens a question on which it is indispensably necessary that clear and sound views should be held by all who would use our language correctly and forcibly. I refer to his abnormal development, so to speak, of the rule that a verb must agree in number with its subject. This rule he thinks is repeatedly violated by the revisers, and he abuses and ridicules them without stint for so doing. He specifies the following instances:

1. "Lay not up for yourselves treasures upon the earth, where moth and rust doth consume." — *Matt. vi.* 19.

2. "Out of the same mouth cometh forth blessing and cursing." — *James iii.* 10.

As to these utterly and inexcusably ungrammatical sentences, of course there can be no difference of opinion.   A ten-year-old boy ought to be ashamed of them ; and their appearance in a work prepared by scholars of such standing as those who constituted the company of revisers, furnishes a striking illustration of the degree to which the study of our own language is neglected in both British and American institutions of learning.   It is most lamentable that such sentences could go through the press without correction.   If all Mr. Moon's illustrations of the error referred to were of this character, one could readily forgive him for almost any display of irritation on discovering them.   But let us see.   He offers further specifications as below:

3. "His face was as the sun, and his feet as pillars of fire." — *Rev. x.* 1.

4. "His feet were as the feet of a bear, and his mouth as the mouth of a lion." — *Rev. xiii.* 2.

5. "Who is my mother and my brethren?" — *Mark iii.* 33.

6. "Is not his mother called Mary? and his brethren, James, and Joseph, and Simon, and Judas?" — *Matt. xiii.* 55.

These sentences are incomplete, certainly;
but it may be questioned whether they are
necessarily equivalent, as Mr. Moon believes,
to writing, in No. 3, "His feet was as pillars of
fire," in No. 4, "His mouth were as the mouth
of a lion," in No. 5, "Who is my brethren?"
and in No. 6, "Is not his brethren?" It seems
to me that the ellipsis is more naturally filled
in, by the mind of the reader, with the verb in
each case in its proper number.

And here is a still more doubtful case:

7. "To whom God was pleased to make known
what is the riches of the glory of this mystery among
the Gentiles, which is Christ in you, the hope of
glory." — *Col. i.* 27.

Mr. Moon is of opinion that the "*is*" in the
last clause refers to "*riches*," and should therefore be "*are.*" It does not seem to me that
the supposed reference is certainly what was
intended; and even if it is, I think that the
clause may be regarded as transposed, the subject of the verb being *Christ*, exactly as in the
sentences "The wages of sin is death" (*Rom. vi.*
23) and "The seal of mine apostleship are ye"

(1 *Cor. ix.* 2) — the verb in each case preceding its subject.   Possibly it would have been better to render the original πλοῦτος by some English word which resembles it in being used in the singular number, "*opulence*," perhaps, or "*wealth*." The matter, at all events, may safely be passed as of rather minor consequence, the error, if error there is, being far from flagrant.

The sentences really important for discussion, in view of Mr. Moon's criticism, are the following :

8. "Among whom also was Dionysius the Areopagite, and a woman named Damaris, and others with them." — *Acts xvii.* 34.

9. "Among whom was Mary Magdalene, and Mary the mother of James and Joses, and the mother of the sons of Zebedee." — *Matt. xxvii.* 56.

10. "Of whom is Hymenæus and Alexander." — 1st *Tim. i.* 20.

11. "Wherein was a golden pot holding the manna, and Aaron's rod that budded, and the tables of the covenant." — *Heb. ix.* 4.

12. "And now abideth faith, hope, love, these three." — 1 *Cor. xiii.* 13.

13. "Where jealousy and faction are, there is confusion and every vile deed." — *James iii.* 16.

14. "Here is the patience and the faith of the saints." — *Rev. xiii.* 10.

15. "On these two commandments hangeth the whole law, and the prophets." — *Matt. xxii.* 40.

16. "Whose is the adoption, and the glory, and the covenants, and the giving of the law, and the service of God, and the promises." — *Rom. ix.* 4.

17. "That ye may be strong to apprehend with all the saints what is the breadth and length and height and depth, and to know the love of Christ." — . *Eph. iii.* 18.

All the above are condemned by Mr. Moon as grossly incorrect; the verb, he thinks, should be plural in every case. It appears to me that the criticism is ill founded. A plural verb would have been correct, assuredly; but it does not necessarily follow that a verb in the singular must be wrong ; and I think that insistence on the plural in such cases would often have the effect of altering — slightly, to be sure, but perceptibly — the shade of meaning intended when (as in at least some of the cases before us) the several subjects of the verb are thought of, not as united in a single conception, but as separate and distinct items. Substantially this explana-

tion of the revisers' language was suggested to
Mr. Moon by one of his reviewers, who said
that " the second substantive is added as a kind
of afterthought " — a suggestion which nearly
threw the critic into a fit.   " *An afterthought of
the Holy Spirit?* " he cries, in shrill hysterics;
" this is dreadful! What *does* Dr. Sanday mean? "
Well, in view of the statements in 1 Cor. i. 14,
15, 16,[1] the supposition of an afterthought in
Scripture seems neither absurd nor blasphemous;
but waiving that point, it must still be clear to
persons not quite so excitable as Mr. Moon
that, whatever view one takes of the inspiration
of the Bible, an inspired writer is just as much
bound by the limitations of language as is any
other, and just as much at liberty, moreover, to
employ figures of rhetoric.   A complete idea
cannot always be presented in a single word,
sometimes not in a single symmetrical phrase;
and a very effective way of making certain classes
of statements is to appear to overlook some
items at first, mentioning them subsequently

---

[1] " I thank God that I baptized none of you, save Crispus
and Gaius; lest any man should say that ye were baptized
into my name.   And I baptized also the household of Ste-
phanas: besides, I know not whether I baptized any other."

one by one as if they had just occurred to the writer as desirable additions or corrections. I think it is in this way, simply and naturally enough, that the ordinary reader will understand the sentences quoted. That is, the effect made on his mind by No. 8 is as if it read: " Among whom was Dionysius the Areopagite, and [also] a woman named Damaris, and others [were] with them." So in No. 12: "And now abideth faith ; [and] hope [abideth] ; [and] love [abideth] ; these three [abide]." Again, in No. 15 : " On these two commandments hangeth the whole law — [yes] and [so do] the prophets [as well]."

In the doxology of the Lord's Prayer — suppressed in the revised version, but mentioned by Mr. Moon as a parallel case of incorrect syntax — I think not only that the translators were justified in following the Greek original by using the verb in the singular, but that the plural would have been positively wrong, as suggesting a connection of thought that was not intended and will not bear analysis. We ask for the blessings solicited " for " (or because) God's is the kingdom, and the power — the sovereignty over even the evil in the universe, and he is able therefore to grant us whatever is good and protect us from whatever is bad. But there is no logic in asking God for help and deliverance *because his is the glory;* and this is just what we should do if we said: "Deliver us from evil, for thine are the kingdom and the power and the glory." This construction would imply that all the subjects of the verb are in the speaker's mind when he begins the clause, and make him say, in effect: "Grant us these blessings, because thine is the glory." As it is, the conclusion seems, to me at least, perfectly clear and reasonable: "Deliver us from evil, for thine is the kingdom [even over the evil], and the power [to save us is thine]; and the glory [is and shall be thine] forever." The object of using language, after all, is to express thought; and while no clear violation of a rule of syntax is to be condoned on the ground that it does not obscure the meaning, yet if the meaning is clear, and the supposed violation is so readily explained away in the reader's mind, there is hardly occasion — to say the least — for extremely severe criticism.

One rather curious blunder into which it is surprising that the revisers fell is repeated by Mr. Moon. They say in their preface (Art. iii. § 2, ¶ 8): "Sometimes the change has been made to avoid tautology"—oblivious (or ignorant) of the manifest fact that there cannot be tautology in an accurate translation if it does not exist in the original. Tautology is the needless repetition of an identical idea in different words; it proceeds from confused thinking, and can neither be aggravated nor ameliorated by changing the phraseology, having indeed nothing to do with any question of the use of language, strictly speaking. The revisers' error on this point is adopted by their critic, who speaks of "verbal repetitions" as equivalent to tautology, and instances these sentences: "From him that hath not, even that which he hath shall be taken away from him" (*Luke xix.* 26), and: "Cast out first the beam out of thine own eye; and then shalt thou see clearly to cast out the mote out of thy brother's eye" (*Matt. vii.* 5). These phrases are unpleasant, certainly; but *they are not tautological;* they have nothing to do with tautology; and it is tolerably certain, notwithstanding the

revisers' fear and Mr. Moon's supposed discovery
that these fears were justified by the issue, that
no case of real tautology exists in any reason-
ably accurate translation of the New Testament.
Were the contrary the case, the responsibility
would assuredly lie further back than with the
translators.

It ought to be said, in general conclusion,
that the revised version is entitled to a good
deal of charity, when judged simply as an
English book. The peculiar difficulties under
which the revisers labored must have been
perplexing and formidable. Their task was not
to make a new translation, but merely to improve
the old. To take an English classic — *any*
English classic — of the beginning of the seventeenth century, and alter its language now,
without thoroughly recasting the whole thing
into the speech of our own day, and without
producing the effect of a patch of new cloth
here and there on the old garment, is a task
from which the most skillful user of our language might well shrink. That the revisers of
1881 secured even a measurable degree of
success in an undertaking at once so arduous

and so delicate, is in a high degree creditable
to their abilities and their judgment; and the
English-speaking public has good reason to
felicitate itself that the final result came anywhere near meeting with general approval. It
is not entirely satisfactory; but one might well
have expected something so much worse!

OLD ENGLISH DICTIONARIES.

A dictionary is not bad reading on the whole. It is much more endurable than a good many of what are called lighter books, and not much more unconnected. . . . In the hands of a patient reader it would form almost a course of study in itself, and very far from a dry one; he would make acquaintance in its pages with a good many English authors to whom no one else is very likely to introduce him; and though this acquaintance would certainly, in one sense, be very superficial, it would not in that respect differ from popular knowledge in general, and would at least have the advantage of being accurate and critical, so far as it went, in point of style. *— Blackwood's Magazine.*

THE history of English lexicography is long and brilliant; it could hardly have been otherwise. The complex and constantly varying structure of our language, perpetually inviting, and perpetually defying, systematic arrangement ; and the circumstances of the people who have used it, scattered as they have been over the whole face of the globe and yet maintaining continued intercourse and corre-

spondence with each other to an extent entirely unparalleled in history, have created a
demand for vocabularies of English very much
more imperative than has existed for those of
any other tongue. Demand creates supply,
and for nearly three centuries a new English
dictionary has appeared about as often as the
leap-year has come round; that is, during the
last 290 years some seventy such works have
been published, not counting revised editions
except when radically remodeled or greatly
enlarged. Many of these books, of course,
are of small importance, but many others are
not only practically very useful, but remarkable, besides, either as monuments of the diligence and the learning of their individual
authors or as showing what marvels can be accomplished by the co-operation of a number
of literary workmen.

The period of 290 years is mentioned as
covering the history of English lexicography,
because the first book which can properly be
called an English dictionary was published in
1604. Lexicographical work had, however,
been done in England, and partly in the lan-

guage of England, nearly a thousand years
before; and even a succinct sketch of the development of the science should notice, at least
as a preliminary stage, the great number of
vocabularies, partly in English and partly in
other tongues, that were welcomed by the literary public from the writing, in the seventh century, of the work on which the Epinal Glossary
was founded, down to Cotgrave's Dictionarie of
the French and English Tongues, dated 1611.
Twenty-five or thirty such works are known to
have been printed, while a much larger number
remained as manuscripts only, a great majority
having been prepared before the invention of
movable types. The earliest of these compilations were mere "glosses" — lists of unfamiliar
terms in particular books, or certain selections
of unfamiliar terms — with interpretations. One
of them, the famous Epinal Glossary, of which
mention has just been made, is especially interesting, as being the very oldest document known
to be now in existence in which the English language is employed. It is a vocabulary of unusual or peculiar Latin (and a few Greek) words,
the equivalents of which are given sometimes in

easier Latin, and sometimes in the English of
those days — not always the English of ours.
It consists of 28 pages of parchment, some of
them badly soiled, but nowhere quite illegible.
On each page are six columns, of which the
first, third and fifth contain, in an approxi-
mation to alphabetical order, the Latin words
to be explained, the interpretations being placed
at the right and forming columns two, four
and six. Phrases occasionally occur, but commonly the author contented himself with rendering in each case a single word by a single
word. The 84 explanatory columns contain
about 3200 entries, of which perhaps a thousand
can be called English, though barely a score of
these would be understood by persons familiar
only with the language as now spoken. It may
be worth while to enumerate these twenty, they
being, as has been mentioned, instances of the
occurrence of terms now in familiar use, in the
oldest document we have in which any English is
to be found, a document written nearly twelve
hundred years ago. It will be noticed that only
two of the twenty have as many as two syllables,
and one of these is a compound. The vener-

able words referred to are: *Garlec, dil, dross, goos, beer* (bier, a litter, not the drink), *malt, ham, bedd, broom* (the plant), *frost, men, handful, storm, spilth, disc, fleah, flint, stream, tin, elm.*

I.

WHAT may be called the first era of purely English lexicography covered practically the seventeenth century. All the dictionaries of our language produced during this period were on the gloss plan, confining themselves to words supposed to be not generally understood. Their authors are nine in number — Cawdrey, Bullokar, Cockeram, Blount, Phillips, Coles, Cocker, one anonymous, and Kersey.

Robert Cawdrey, the first of all, began the great work by issuing a small book with a large title: "A Table Alphabeticall, conteyning and teaching the true writing, and understanding of hard usual English wordes, borrowed from the Hebrew, Greeke, Latine, or French, &c., with the interpretation thereof by plaine English words, gathered for the benefit & helpe of ladies, gentlewomen, or any other unskilfull persons, whereby they may the more easilie and better understand many hard English wordes, which they shall heare or read in scriptures, sermons, or elsewhere, and also be made able to use the same aptly themselves. *Legere, et non intelligere, neglegere est* — as good not read, as not to understand. At London, printed by I. R. for Edmund Weaver, & are to be sold at his shop at the great north doore of Paules Church: 1604." It will be seen that the author's name does not appear on the title-page, but it is signed to a letter of dedication that follows. The persons that he had chiefly in mind must have been "unskilfull" indeed, for he judges it needful to add this caution: "If thou be desirous (gentle reader) rightly and readily to understand, and profit by this table, and such like, then thou must learn the alphabet, to wit, the order of the letters as they stand, perfectly without book, and where every letter standeth: as (*b*) neere the beginning, (*n*) about the middest, and (*t*) toward the end."

Twelve years after the appearance of Cawdrey's "Table," namely in 1616, Dr. John Bullokar issued his " English Expositour, or

Compleat Dictionary, teaching the interpretation of the hardest words, and most useful
terms of art used in our language," and said
to contain 5080 entries. A copy of the sixth
edition of this work, dated 1680, may be seen
at the New York State Library in the capi-
tol at Albany — a 24mo of about 290 pages.
One definition, not badly expressed for the
time, caught my eye in looking it over. This is
that of the term *heretick*, which Dr. Bullokar
explains thus : " He that maketh his own choice,
what points of religion he will believe, and what
he will not believe." The author was no friend
to vain repetitions, and when he has dealt with,
for instance, an adjective, he generally leaves it
to the common-sense of the reader to divine for
himself the meanings of the allied noun and verb.
" If," he remarks, "the adjective *crude* signifies
raw, the substantive *crudity* must signify raw-
ness, and so contrarily." Perhaps he carried his
rule too far, but the main principle seems to
have reason, and if it had been adopted at least
in part by modern dictionary makers — to the
exclusion of such utterly superfluous entries
as " *bottle-ale* " in Webster, " *madwoman* " in

Worcester and "*codliver oil*" in the Century, the
dictionary-using public would have had cause
for gratitude.   But the most characteristic feature of Bullokar's book, and one hardly to be
commended, is an index "wherein the vulgar
[or common] words are prefixed in an alphabetical order before the others [that is, the
grander words of foreign derivation] as a ready
direction for the finding them out," assisting
writers to turn their plain, succinct English into
high-flown and almost always longer terms, to
the manifest injury of their style.   The work
has also a sort of brief cyclopædia, "containing
a summary of the most memorable things and
famous persons."   The last paragraph of the
doctor's preface is worth copying:

"Those virtuous and well addicted persons, who,
rather for want of opportunity than generous inclin-
ation, not having had the fortune to attain to the
knowledge of any other than the mother language,
are yet studiously desirous to read those learned and
eloquent treatises which from their native original
have been rendered English (of which sort, thanks
to the company of painful translators, we have not
a few), have here a volume fit for their purpose, as

carefully designed for their assistance ; and to such, and only such, we recommend it, and that with this benediction, live long, industrious reader, advance in knowledge and be happy."

Seven years after Bullokar, 1623, appeared " The English Dictionary, or an Interpreter of Hard English Words," by H[enry] C[ockeram], Gent. This writer is best remembered for his exhortation to the " gentle reader " to " have a care to search every word according to the true orthography thereof; as for *Physiognomie* in the letter *P*, not in *F*, for *cynicall* in *Cy*, not *Ci*." His horror of what he calls " vulgar " words is also a distinguishing feature. Thus he condemns the adjective *rude* and tells us to say " agresticall; " also the verb *to weede*, for which he would substitute the pleasing terms to " *sarculate*," to " *diruncinate*," or to " *averuncate*." The work ran to at least nine editions.

At about the middle of the century under review, namely, in 1656, appeared Thomas Blount's " Glossographia, or a dictionary interpreting the hard words of whatsoever language now used in our refined English tongue; with etymologies, definitions and historical observa-

tions on the same." It is largely composed of
foreign and technical words, but includes historical and geographical names also, as well as
many words now at least (possibly not then) of
daily use. One is *stepmother*, so-called, Blount
thought, " because she steps in instead of a
mother by marrying the son or daughter's
father; a mother-in-law." The work " is chiefly
intended," says a note to the reader in the edition of 1670, " for the more-knowing women,
and less-knowing men; or indeed for all such of
the unlearned, who can but find in an alphabet
the word they understand not; yet I think I
may modestly say the best of scholars may in
some part or other be obliged by it." A fifth
edition, considerably enlarged, appeared in 1681,
making a duodecimo of 710 pages, which are
duly numbered on the present plan.

In 1658, Edward Phillips (nephew of John
Milton) issued the first edition of his " New
World of Words, or a Universal English Dictionary, containing the proper significations and
derivations of all words from other languages
* * * as now made use of in our English tongue,
together with the definitions of all those terms

that conduce to the understanding of any of the
arts or sciences, * * * to which is added the interpretations of proper names * * * as also the
sum of all the most remarkable mythology and
history, deduced from the names of persons
eminent in either; and likewise the geographical descriptions of the chief countries and cities
in the world — a work very necessary for stran-
gers, as well as our own countrymen, for the
right understanding of what they discourse,
write or read." One definition seems worth
copying. "Acid in chymistry," it says, "signifies that sharp salt, or that potential and dis-
solving fire which is in all mixed bodies, and
gives 'em being. Of acids, vitriol is the chiefest,
sea salt next to that." Phillips copied very
largely from Blount, blunders and all, and added
a considerable number of errors of his own.
Among other things, he defines *gallon* as a
measure containing two quarts; *quaver* as "a
measure of time in music, being the half of a
crotchet, as a crotchet is the half of a quaver;"
contemptuous as synonymous with *contemptible*
and meaning "worthy of scorn;" *ember-week*
as "the week before Lent;" and he men-

tions *Nazareth* as " the place where Christ was born."

Next came, in 1677, Elisha Coles, " schoolmaster and teacher of the tongue to foreigners," with " an English dictionary explaining the difficult terms that are used in divinity, husbandry, physic, philosophy, law, navigation, mathematics and other arts and sciences " — claimed to contain almost thirty thousand entries. A new feature in this work is a list of what we should now call homonyms, pairs (or triplets) of words having the same sound, but different spellings and meanings. The preface criticises severely the productions of previous lexicographers.

Early in the eighteenth century, 1704, was issued, posthumously, the English Dictionary of Edward Cocker, an unimportant work, though several times republished, with alterations and additions by John Hawkins, who felicitated himself on his success by printing as a separate line on the title-page the words: " The Like never yet Extant."

In 1707 appeared the anonymous " Glossographia Anglicana Nova, a dictionary inter-

preting such hard words as are at present used
in the English tongue." It has a number of
wood-cuts illustrating definitions of heraldic
terms, this being the earliest appearance of any
sort of pictorial illustrations in an English lexicon.   The author, like Phillips, had his own
idea on the subject of acids, his statement being
as follows: "Acids are those bodies which produce the taste of sharpness or sourness, caused
from the particles of those bodies being sharp-
pointed and piercing."

The first period of our English lexicography
may be said to have closed in 1708, with the
appearance of J[ohn] K[ersey]'s "New English Dictionary, or a compleat collection of the
most proper and significant words, and terms of
art commonly used in the language, * * * for
the benefit of young scholars, tradesmen, arti-
ficers, foreigners and the female sex." It is
doubtful, however, whether this work is not
almost entitled to be counted as the first of
the second period, for in design, though perhaps not in execution, it goes rather beyond
the gloss plan. It professes to omit obsolete,
barbarous and foreign words, and originally

included a number of such familiar terms as *bird-cage*, *apple-tree* and *pigeon-house*. These particular compounds, however, and probably many others of the same class, were wisely omitted from the second edition, a duodecimo of about 300 pages issued in 1713, and of which the author modestly remarks that "the entire work (as it is now brought to perfection) must needs give ample content to the public."

It has seemed worth while to describe these works at some length, considering that they make up what may be termed the incunabula of English lexicography. Cawdrey, first on the list of their authors, turned up absolutely virgin soil, and each of the eight who came after him is distinguished by a good deal of originality. Their books are not only, in most cases, incomparably smaller than our modern dictionaries, but they have a very different style — they are conversational, almost chatty, and yet there are wide differences in tone, so to speak, among them. They constitute a class of literature which is distinctly of its own kind and well deserves separate preservation and study.

II.

A SECOND period, transitional between that of the glosses which preceded it and that of the modern dictionary, supposed to contain the whole language, was introduced in 1721 by the publication of the great work of Nathan Bailey, in which it was for the first time attempted to include " the generality of words in the English tongue." This book had a long life, which it well deserved, running through at least twenty-seven editions, many of them involving extensive alterations.   Like the dictionaries of the present day, it was offered at different times in various forms and sizes, sometimes in one volume and sometimes in two.   The most noted edition is the folio of 1730, a volume of nearly 900 pages, 9 inches by $13\frac{1}{2}$, a copy of which, with blank leaves inserted, was used by Johnson as the foundation of his labors.   Bailey's work is remarkable also as marking the accented syllables of the words — which no previous author had done, and as containing a " collection of proverbs, with their explanation and illustra-

tion." Thus under the entry *swallow* we find
noted the adage " one swallow does not make
a summer," with the following explanation,
which certainly ought to make the matter tolerably clear:

"All the false as well as the foolish conclusions
from a particular to an universal truth fall under the
censure of this proverb. It teaches that as he that
guesses at the course of the year by the flight of
one single bird is very liable to be mistaken in his
conjecture ; so that a man cannot be denominated
rich from one single piece of money in his pocket,
nor accounted universally good from the practice of
one single virtue, nor temperate because he is stout,
nor liberal because he is exactly just ; that one day
cannot render a man completely happy in point of
time, nor one action consummate his glory in point
of valor. In short, the moral of it is, that the right
way of judging of things, beyond imposition and
fallacy, is not from particulars, but universals."

Bailey was followed, in 1724, by Hawkins'
enlargement of Cocker; in 1735 by Defoe's
"Compleat English Dictionary"—an unimportant work with a consequential title—and
by Dyche & Pardon, whose book was "intended

for the information of the unlearned, * * * not only in orthography * * * but in writing coherently and correctly, the want whereof is universally complained of among the fair sex;"— not very gallant, these old lexicographers. In 1737 came Sparrow, with the " New English Dictionary," published anonymously; in 1741, Daniel Fenning, the "Royal English Dictionary;" in 1749, Benjamin Martin, "A New Universal English Dictionary;" and in 1753, John Wesley, the clergyman, who naturally enough defines *Methodist* as "one that lives according to the method laid down in the Bible," and who put on his title-page this "N. B. —The author assures you, he thinks this is the best English dictionary in the world." None of these works has historical importance; Bailey will ever stand as the only name worth remembering between Kersey and Johnson.

MODERN DICTIONARIES: WHICH IS THE BEST?

The difference between the dictionaries which are now in use, and are daily coming into greater use — for the end is not yet — and those which were received as standards when Johnson and his hacks began to classify and explain the language in accordance with the rules of the classical languages, is the difference between history as written by Rollin, and Hume, and Smollett and Goldsmith in England, and as it has been written in our time by Froude, and Macaulay, and Freeman, and Gardiner, and other conscientious students of State papers and ancient correspondence. Our philologists, like our historians, have grown critical, and if there ever was a period when the study of words can be said to have ranked among, or even to have approximated to, the exact sciences, it is now. — *New York Mail & Express, Editorial.*

I.

THE third or modern period of the development of English lexicography dates from the appearance of the Johnson of 1755 — a massive folio in two volumes, on which its great author worked hard for seven years (it is a wonder it did not take him longer), and which, though it brought him very little money, he had the great satisfaction of seeing received with the warm enthusiasm which its unique merits amply deserved. It is a good deal the fashion to make merry over Johnson and his definitions, and certain entries are undoubtedly provocative of mirth, though not always exactly at the expense of the author, for in many cases he knew perfectly well what he was about, and deliberately intended using his lexicography as a means for expressing his personal opinions — prejudices and notions, if you like to call them so — no matter what anybody might think about it. Instances of this kind are almost too familiar to quote. A *patron*, he says, is "commonly a wretch who supports with insolence and is paid with flattery;" a *pension* "in England is generally understood to mean pay given to a state hireling for treason to his country," and a *pensioner* is "a slave of state hired to obey his master," while *patriot* is a term "sometimes used for a factious disturber of the government." A *Tory* is "one who

8

adheres to the ancient constitution of the state;" a *Whig* is "the name of a faction," and a *Puritan* is "a sectary pretending to eminent purity of religion." *Excise* is "a hateful tax levied upon commodities, and adjudged by wretches."

In other cases, the only explanation that can be given of the extraordinary statements made is sheer carelessness and inattention. If we knew not the author, what kind of a sloven must we think him to have been who could define *pink* as "a color used by painters," and *brown* as "a color compounded of black and any other color"? In some cases again, as in *ferret*, "a kind of rat," and *pastern*, "the leg of a horse," the "ignorance, madam, sheer ignorance" that he was himself so ready to admit, is indisputable. In others, his Johnsonese got decidedly the better of his English, as when he tells us that *network* is "anything reticulated or decussated, at equal distances, with interstices between the intersections." In other cases we find the personal element verging on the side of pathos, as where *Grub Street* is defined as "a street much inhabited by writers of small histories, dictionaries and temporary poems; whence any mean production is called 'Grub Street,'"—and *lexicographer* as "a writer of dictionaries, a harmless drudge." The pathos rises into real eloquence in the elaborate preface to the great work, a composition which Horne Tooke, Johnson's bitterest enemy and detractor in the literary world, said he could never read without tears. The final paragraph runs thus:

"In this work, when it shall be found that much is omitted, let it not be forgotten that much likewise is performed ; and though no book was ever spared out of tenderness to the author, and the world is little solicitous to know whence proceeded the faults of that which it condemns ; yet it may gratify curiosity to inform it, that the English Dictionary was written with little assistance of the learned, and without any patronage of the great ; not in the soft obscurities of retirement, or under the shelter of academic bowers, but amidst inconvenience and distraction, in sickness and in sorrow. It may repress the triumph of malignant criticism to observe, that if our language is not here fully displayed, I have only failed in an attempt which no human powers have hitherto completed.   If the lexicons of ancient tongues, now immutably fixed and comprised in a few volumes, be yet, after the toil of successive ages, inadequate and delusive; if the aggregated knowledge, and co-operating diligence of the Italian academicians, did not secure them from the censure of Beni, if the embodied critics of France, when fifty years had been spent upon their work, were obliged to change its œconomy, and give their second edition another form, I may surely be contented without the praise of perfection, which, if I could obtain, in this gloom of solitude, what would it avail me? I have protracted my work till most of those whom I wished to please have sunk into the grave, and success and miscarriage are empty sounds: I therefore dismiss it with frigid tranquillity, having little to fear or hope from censure or from praise."

With all its faults, Johnson's dictionary was a work of entirely unprecedented excellence. Beside coming far nearer than Bailey to including every word recognized at his time as good English, he first introduced citations from standard authors to support his definitions, and both his citations and his definitions have been found extremely useful to subsequent lexicographers, insomuch that most of them have copied both,

with great freedom; and notwithstanding the
large number of the dictionaries that have since
appeared, Johnson's, after nearly a century and
a half, is only just now becoming obsolete. At
the great spelling matches that excited this
country less than twenty years ago, it may be
remembered that the rules explicitly provided
that any spelling recognized by Johnson should
be regarded as correct.

The limits of this paper will hardly permit
any real attempt to trace satisfactorily the development of our popular English dictionary from
Johnson down. In the twenty years following
the appearance of his first edition, more than
a dozen authors tried their hands, without greatly
advancing the work — Jas. Buchanan, "A New
Spelling English Dictionary," 1757; J. Peyton,
"A New Vocabulary," 1759; D. Bellamy, "En-
glish Dictionary," 1760; J. N. Scott, "Bailey's
Dictionary Revised," 1764; Daniel Farro, "The
Royal British Grammar and Vocabulary," 1764;
William Johnston, "A Pronouncing and Spelling
Dictionary," 1764; John Entick, "A Spelling
Dictionary of the English Language," 1764; J.
Baskerville, "A Vocabulary or Pocket Diction-

ary," 1765; Wm. Rider, "Universal English Dictionary," 1766; J. Seally, "The London Spelling Dictionary," 1771; Fred'k Barlow, "A Complete English Dictionary," 1772; Wm. Kenrick, "A New Dictionary," 1773, — in which work I believe one step forward was taken, by the use, for the first time, of figures over the vowels to indicate their sounds; Jas. Barclay, "A Complete and Universal English Dictionary," 1774; and one or two anonymous writers. At 1775 we must pause a moment, for in that year appeared the memorable work of John Ash, memorable as containing (in addition to the interesting statements that *esoteric* is "an incorrect spelling" of *exoteric*, and that Gawain was sister to King Arthur) perhaps the most extraordinary blunder in all lexicography — his noted etymology of the word *curmudgeon*. Johnson suggested that the derivation might be from the French *cœur méchant* (meaning *evil heart*), and credits an unknown correspondent with the idea — that is, he inserts the note: "It is a vicious manner of pronouncing *cœur méchant*, French — an unknown correspondent." In Ash's book we find the amazing statement that *curmudgeon* is "from the French *cœur*, unknown, and *méchant*, a correspondent"! Think of the qualification for work at English lexicography that a man must have possessed whose knowledge of the most elementary French was so absolutely non-existent, and whose lack of common sense was so stupendous, as to render this sort of performance possible! And the best of it is that in the "advertisement" prefixed to the work, we are assured that in the derivations from other languages "special attention has been given to the mere English scholar by a proper analysis and full explanation of the originals"!

Ash was followed, in the same year, by Perry, and then by an anonymous "pocket dictionary" (1779), and in 1780 by Sheridan, who first, as I believe, re-spelled words in order to indicate the pronunciation. Then came Harwood's revision of Bailey (1782), Lemon (1783), Fry's "Vocabulary of Difficult Words" (1784), Picard (1790), and the next year (1791) John Walker with his "Critical Pronouncing Dictionary," which ran through thirty or forty editions and still retains its place as an important authority, at least on questions of orthoëpy, within the memory of persons now living. Walker paid little attention to etymology, and "with respect to the explanation of words, except in very few instances, * * * scrupulously followed Johnson," whose dictionary, he adds, "has been deemed lawful plunder by every subsequent lexicographer." The great feature of his work is the attention paid in it to pronunciation, an elaborate treatise on that subject being prefixed, together with certain rather amusing "rules to be observed by the natives of Scotland, Ireland and London, for avoiding their respective peculiarities."

Walker was followed by William Scott (1797), Stephen Jones[1] (1798), Fulton & Knight[1] (1802), William Perry[1] (1805), Thos. Browne, (1806), Wm. Enfield (1807), W. F. Mylius (18—), Christopher Earnshaw (*circ.* 1815), R. S. Jameson[1] (1827), Saml. Maunder (1830), David Booth (1835), James Knowles (1835), B. H.

---

[1] These authors, as well as Walker and Sheridan, are the orthoëpists cited in the "synopsis of words differently pronounced by different authorities," in the early editions of Webster.

Smart (1836), sundry anonymous writers, and various revisions and enlargements of older works, of which much the most important is the Todd's Johnson of 1818; but the next contribution of real and original value to the science, in England, was not made until 1836, when Charles Richardson, "firmly persuaded that * * * a new dictionary ought to be written, and of a very different kind indeed from anything yet attempted anywhere," endeavored to supply the want. The great desideratum in such a work, he thought, was "a collection of usages quoted from, in general, our best English authors, and those usages explained to suit the quotations; and those explanations including within them a portion of the sense pertaining to other words in the sentence." The citations, accordingly, constitute the distinctive feature of the work. They were collected with great diligence and in much abundance and variety, a period of about five centuries having been reviewed, beginning with Robert of Gloucester, contemporaneous with Edward the First, and ending about the year 1800. Richardson's work has always been of high interest to schol-

ars, and is the first not founded on Johnson;
but the vocabulary, the definitions, and the
marks indicating the orthoëpy, are alike insuffi-
cient to meet the popular demand, and it has
never, perhaps, been fully appreciated. It
makes two quarto volumes, 2224 pages in all,
three columns to the page, resembling quite
closely in dimensions the recent editions of
Webster's Unabridged.

Following Richardson came Reid (1844),
Sullivan (1847), Boag (1848), Craig (1849), and
then (in 1850) Ogilvie, with the first edition
of the great Imperial, which was afterwards
revised and materially improved by Annandale,
was generally regarded for a long time as the
standard authority in Great Britain, and had
the honor of serving as a sort of foundation
for the much greater Century. It may gratify
American pride to know that the Imperial was
avowedly based on our own Webster, which is
spoken of in the preface as not only superior
to Richardson and Todd's Johnson, "but superior to every other dictionary hitherto published." In its latest form (1882), the Imperial
makes four large octavo volumes of seven or

eight hundred pages each, and contains about
130,000 entries, illustrated by more than three
thousand engravings. In the length of its
vocabulary, the extent of its definitions, and
the number and excellence of its illustrations,
it far outshone any similar work previously
issued in Great Britain, being indeed the first
to combine largely the features of a cyclopædia
—which explains things—with those of a
dictionary—which defines words; the sub-title
"A Complete Encyclopædic Lexicon, Literary,
Scientific and Technological," is fully justified
by the contents.

The works of Wright and Clarke (both published in 1855) and of Cooley and Nuttall
(both in 1861) detracted little from the fame
of the Imperial. Latham's Todd's Johnson
(1866) was a more important work and long
enjoyed great popularity in England. A much
more formidable rival to the Imperial, however,
—meeting it exactly on its own ground—is
the Encyclopædic, the first volume of which
appeared in 1879 and the seventh and last in
'88, labor having begun on it as far back as
'72. This is a very extensive work, containing

nearly 6,000 pages and about 180,000 words or headings. It carries the encyclopædic features even beyond the point reached by the Imperial, and is fully illustrated and handsomely printed. Some omissions are a little remarkable, especially perhaps that of the word *fair* as signifying an exhibition — a use of the word now quite common in Great Britain as well as the United States; and *sweeny*, a disease of the horse. (The latter term, however, seems to be missing in all dictionaries except the International, the Century and the Standard.) A still more curious feature in the Encyclopædic is the remarkable blunder of using the word *molasses* as a plural —"a tank having a perforated bottom, through which the molasses escape,"— art. "*Tiger*," II., 2. This dictionary was republished in Philadelphia in 1894, "Americanized" in respect to a number of its definitions, and bound in the more convenient form of four volumes, each containing some 1340 pages of about the size of the International.

Another most excellent British work, though of very different character, is Stormonth's, first issued in October, 1871, and nine times repub-

lished, the latest form being the large-type
edition of 1884. It is an extremely sound and
scholarly work, though well adapted to the
needs of the general public, a great wealth of
trustworthy information being condensed into
small compass, and very clearly as well as
briefly stated. It has no quotations and no
engravings, but it is questionable whether either
of these features has really proper place in a
dictionary of language, strictly so called; and
it is not too much to say that for the ordinary
purposes of hasty reference, when encyclopædic information is not sought for, a person
having Stormonth's dictionary at hand will in
only exceptional cases and at long intervals
regret the absence of any other. It represents,
in fact, the very highest development of the
English word-book, pure and simple.

The first English dictionary published in
this country was the work, strangely enough,
of a man really named Samuel Johnson, Jr. —
a small book, intended for schools, and issued
just before the opening of the present century.
Next, in 1800, came Elliott's, Mr. Johnson's
name appearing as co-editor, while among those

who signed commendations of the value of the work was Noah Webster.

Of other American dictionaries, only four require notice, and Worcester's may be most briefly disposed of. The author of this noble work came first before the public in 1827, with a revised edition of Todd's Johnson combined with Walker, but only three years later issued his own " Comprehensive Dictionary," and in 1835 his " Elementary Dictionary for Common Schools." These were both small works, his more ambitious "Universal and Critical Dictionary" not coming out until 1846, and his main work, as we have it now, not until 1860, though his earlier books had been in the mean time more than once reissued with considerable enlargement. In its final form, Worcester's dictionary is in a high degree creditable to the scholarship, the judgment and the industry of its distinguished author. It was long the favorite of the more cultured users of such books, who appreciated the great care which Dr. Worcester always employed to ascertain and record the best practice in both spelling and pronunciation. But, even with the inconvenient addition of the Supplement of 1881, Worcester is now too far behind the times to render the greatest practical service. I have myself happened to notice, from time to time, the absence of a considerable number of words and uses of words now quite common. Examples are: *Furore, coral* of lobster, *mat* of a picture frame, *macramé, ensilage, casket* in the sense of coffin, *rep, boycott, toboggan, apiculture, skewbald, sweeny, muley, dynamo-electric, pigeon English, solid-colored, jobmaster, ninepence, hectograph, self-contained, maverick* — and the list could doubtless be run up into the hundreds, by comparison with later works. It still contains, moreover, what Dr. Webster would call the "nonsensical" word *phantomnation*, defined as "illusion" — a word which is not a word, being taken by misapprehension from a passage of Pope, as quoted by one Richard Paul Jodrell in a work called "Philology of the English Language," issued in 1820 as a sort of supplement to Johnson's dictionary. The passage is:

These solemn vows and holy offerings paid
To all the phantom nations of the dead.
Odyssey, X. 627.

Jodrell had a great fancy for printing compound words solid, without a hyphen to indicate
their component parts. So he wrote "phan-
tomnations" as one word, and Dr. Worcester
took it up. From him it passed to Webster's
Unabridged (though it does not appear in the
International), to the Imperial (though it does
not appear in the Century), and to the Encyclopædic — showing the remarkable vitality that
a simple blunder, which might originally have
been avoided by a little care, will sometimes
possess. Unless Worcester's dictionary be entirely revised and greatly extended, it seems
certain very shortly to follow Johnson into " in-
nocuous desuetude " so far as practical service
is concerned, though, like Johnson also, it will
forever remain an interesting — yes, and an
imposing — monument of the achievements of
the past.

And now we come to Webster, first published, a small book, in 1806, and again — in
another form, specially intended for school use
— in 1807. These works were, however, only
preliminary to the greater undertaking, the well-
known "Unabridged," which appeared in two

volumes, quarto, in 1828, and was reissued, enlarged, in two volumes, large octavo, in 1840 — this being the last edition with which Webster himself had anything to do. In 1847 appeared, under the editorship of Prof. Goodrich, a new edition, in the single square-volume style now so familiar; in 1859 another; in 1864 another, edited by Dr. Noah Porter, to which was added, in 1879, an extended supplement; and in 1890, the great Webster International, a work on which many of the ablest minds of the world were long employed, and on which no less than $300,000 is said to have been expended by the publishers before a single copy was printed.

To avoid danger of misapprehension, one must choose words very carefully in pronouncing any sort of critical opinion of Webster's dictionary. In its earlier editions it was unreasonably denounced; in its later forms it has been in certain respects greatly over-valued. A popular writer has said that in its original form it was something for Americans to laugh at and be ashamed of — which is just about as true as the pronunciamento of a great British philolo-

gist to the effect that Johnson's dictionary was
a disgrace to the language. Abuse like this only
pillories the abusers, in after time, as either extremely rash and inconsiderate in their statements, culpably ignorant or careless of essential
facts, or controlled by some sort of bias or
unreasonable prejudice. On the other hand, it
savors of absurdity to quote Webster as "authority" on any doubtful point, either in the
minor matters of orthoëpy and spelling, or in
the far more important matter of definition.
The plan on which the author at first proceeded,
and the plans on which every revision of his
work has been conducted, were such as absolutely to take the book out of the class of authorities, properly speaking, if by authority is
understood, as I think it clearly should be, the
representation of what is recognized as the best
actual practice. Dr. Webster's original idea
was to exhibit the language, not as it then existed, but as he thought it should be; the plan
pursued since his death has been to admit every
sort of vagary that has attained any degree of
general circulation, insomuch that it has been
said that there is no slovenly or improper use

of an English word ever heard in decent society
for which the authority of Webster cannot be
cited. The statement does the dictionary in-
justice; it is not meant to be an authority, in
the sense in which the word is used; and yet I
think there can be no doubt that on account of
the general misconception that has prevailed on
this point, and the consequent idea that anything admitted to Webster must be correct, the
dictionary, with its enormous popularity, has
been a potent agent in injuring our language.
By injuring, is meant, rendering the English
tongue less clearly intelligible and definite, so
that it is now in some degree an inferior instru-
ment for conveying thought from man to man
to what it would presumably have been, without
this influence. Variations in spelling and in pronunciation are of little moment, from the stand-
point of practical daily life; the admission of
new words, no matter how "slangy" or ill-
formed, is very often a positive gain; and the
use of old words in figurative and rhetorical
senses naturally connected with the original
significance is of course a privilege which any
one may freely take, with a clear conscience.

But the blundering use of words to signify what they do not mean tends just so far to confuse communication between persons using the language thus treated, and to hasten the ultimate destruction of the language itself. The recognition, in a book like Webster's dictionary, of pretty nearly every sort of erroneous use of common words that the editors have observed, without warning the reader of the impropriety of such use, naturally induces the supposition that the lexicographer not only explains the error, but lends it his authority as correct, thus aiding and abetting in the process of depraving the tongue. And all this may be said, and said emphatically, without the slightest disrespect to the ability, the learning, the energy, the achievements, of the great scholars who have collaborated in producing the inestimably useful work under review. Many blessings for which we cannot be too grateful have connected with them features that may render them susceptible of inflicting very serious injury, if unskillfully used. Such a blessing is Webster's dictionary.

Of works designed for popular circulation, only two others call for remark. The first and greatest is the magnificent Century, a dictionary which not only has 215,000 words, but which comes near to being a cyclopædia as well, and which is almost beyond criticism in its execution, literary, artistic and mechanical. This work is too recent, and at the same time too well known, to need extended description or eulogy. But it may be proper to note, as one of its minor merits most likely to escape observation, that the editors have been more careful than those of Webster to warn the reader not to quote their work as authority for the improper uses of terms which they explain. Excellent examples of the difference may be found in the two words *centenary* and *demean*. Each dictionary recognizes the fact that the former, *centenary*, which means merely *hundredth*, is often employed as if it had something to do with the Latin *annum*, and were therefore descriptive of a period of a hundred years; and Webster, dropping no hint that such use is a mistake, might naturally be quoted as "authorizing" it, whereas the Century distinctly informs the reader that the practice referred to has arisen from confusing *centenary* with the quite different word *centennial*. Simi-

larly, we find in Webster, among other definitions of the verb *demean*, these: "To debase,
to lower, to degrade." A note, to be sure, is
added that this use of the word "is probably
due to a false etymology;" but no hint is given
that such use is not now universally approved,
and (as is the case of *centenary* for *centennial*)
Webster might therefore naturally enough be
quoted as "authorizing" it. The Century says
that the verb *to demean*, when used in the sense
referred to, is "illegitimate in origin, inconvenient in use," and "avoided by scrupulous writers." If people will persist in the mistake, they
certainly cannot quote the Century as supporting them, and they may so quote Webster. The
latter therefore is to some extent responsible
for the injury to the language which follows
every such error; the former is not. It must be
regretfully added, however, that in the case of
one wretched vulgarism — chiefly confined, I
believe, to the northern United States — the
Century is worse than Webster. This is the use
of the verb *claim* as meaning merely to *assert*,
where there is really no claiming in the matter.
Webster marks it as "colloquial," thus giving it

at least a qualified disapproval; the Century says only that this is "a common use, regarded by many as inelegant," thus implying that many other persons are of a contrary opinion, and that the expression may well enough pass muster. The explanation lies probably in the curious fact that Prof. Whitney, the editor of the Century, has been caught in this blunder himself — it occurs at least twice in his " Elements of English Pronunciation " — and he was therefore naturally loth to characterize it as he must of course know that it deserves, in his dictionary. One other oddity of this great work, not an error, however, has amused some readers, — the insertion, in the article " *question*," of the suggestive entry, "popping the question — see pop!"

And finally, we have the Standard dictionary, published in 1894 — a very handsome book, containing about 1100 pages somewhat larger than those of the International and somewhat smaller, but more closely printed, than those of the Century. Like the last-named work, it is constructed on the cyclopædia plan, and it indeed far surpasses, in certain cyclopædic features — as in the articles *apple, constellation, dog, fowl*, and particularly the extended treatises under *coin* and *geology* — the Century itself. To my own thinking, this great elaboration of special topics in a dictionary of English words is rather undesirable. The Century, it seems to me, goes quite far enough in that direction, including as it does about all the general information in regard to things (as distinguished from words) that one would be likely to go to a dictionary to find; and much of the added matter of the Standard — such as the two and a half columns devoted to the description of hundreds of varieties of the apple, with their relative advantages for different divisions of the country — seems almost ludicrously out of place in a work that belongs, after all, to the department of philology. It is moreover extremely difficult to preserve due proportion between different parts of the work, if minute elaboration of the kind referred to is indulged in; and the editors of the Standard have not invariably succeeded beyond criticism. To the article *geology*, for instance, they devote considerably more than two pages, inserting a complicated and doubtless very valuable chart of the crust of the earth and its fossils, while the (as one would suppose) at least equally interesting science of *astronomy* is dismissed with a mere definition. Why not give us at least a map of the solar system?

Not only, however, is the Standard rather ill-proportioned in its information about things ; it is also — a graver fault — somewhat inconsistent with itself in the important matter of its treatment of a large class of words — the words that are often misused. In some cases, as in the application of the term *buck* to the male of the sheep (distinctly " authorized " by the International), it goes to the extreme of ignoring the error altogether ; in others, as in *demean* in the sense of *debase*, it follows the Century by noting the usage but marking it as wrong ; in still others, as *centenary* for *centennial*, *aggravate* for *irritate*, and *circumstance* for *event*, it is as bad as Webster, giving the reader no warning that these uses of the words will mark him as at least careless of the finer proprieties of speech ; and it gives place with seeming approval to the absurd vocable *helpmeet*. A dictionary of English should do one thing or the other. It may record without comment all common words and all common uses of words, proceeding on the conception that a lexicographer is a compiler and an explainer, not a critic; but if the attempt is made to distinguish right usage from that which must tend to the deterioration of the language as a vehicle of thought, care should be taken not to pass gross blunders without characterizing them as what they are.

It is now a pleasure to hasten to admit that these defects in the Standard are not of a nature to disturb one user of English dictionaries out of a hundred; and to say emphatically that the solid merits of the work are remarkable and distinguished. Greater care seems to have been taken in its preparation than was ever taken before, to secure on every even minute point the best matured opinions of the best equipped experts ; and as the definitions are generally models of conciseness and precision, one can hardly ever fail to obtain from its pages the fact that he seeks, quickly, fully, accurately, and with every reason to depend on the correctness of the information furnished. A single illustration may be given. The word *abacus*, as used in the 35th chapter of Ivanhoe to designate

the staff of office of the grand master of the
Knights Templars, appears in no previous dictionary ; it is found in the Standard, and not
only that, but the reader is informed that Scott
erred in using it, the proper term being *baculus*.
A dictionary that goes so far as to indicate a
trifling slip like this, which may probably have
occurred once only in our literature, may safely
be presumed not to omit much that the most
inquisitive reader is likely to wish to find.   The
Standard will certainly prove of immense value,
and exceedingly convenient for ready reference.
Moreover, its wood engravings compare favor-
ably with those in the Century, and its colored
plates are more beautiful than anything of the
kind that was ever attempted before.   Altogether, it is a work of which the country that
gave it birth has good reason to be proud.

With the Standard, closes for the present the
list of English dictionaries designed for popular
use ; but the greatest dictionary that was ever
compiled of any language is still to be mentioned — a dictionary, however, intended only
for students and scholars.   This is the badly
named " New English Dictionary on Historical

Principles, founded mainly on the materials collected by the [British] Philological Society, and
edited by Dr. James A. H. Murray,"—or, to
adopt the short title generally used, the "Murray Philological." It will probably make some
nine volumes, each of them three quarters as
thick as the Webster International and having considerably larger pages, quite as closely
printed and no space taken up by illustrations, —
accommodating an immense quantity of matter.
But the bulk of this dictionary, enormous as
it is, must be regarded as merely an incidental
feature, so to speak, of its unique and unap-
proached value. The main point is that we
have in it a complete history of every English
word from its appearance to our own time, with
full explanation of its etymology, its original
meaning in English, and the changes in form,
use or significance which it may have undergone,
accompanied with citations, historically arranged,
and so stated as to render reference extremely
easy. An illustration will show the working of
the plan. The word *by-product*, common as it
now is, had appeared in no previous dictionary.
Yet Dr. Murray found it in a work published in

1857 — Eliza Acton's "English Bread Book":
"German yeast in many distilleries forms an
important by-product." Quotations are added
from a scientific work issued in 1879 and a London newspaper of August 24, 1882, the last
being perhaps considered sufficient to indicate
that the term had then become a part of our
every-day speech. Or take the noun *American*.
This is defined, first, as "an aborigine of the
American continent, now called an 'American
Indian.'" Four apt quotations follow, the first
dated 1578 and indicating the very earliest use
of the word that has been discovered, and the
last 1777, being the latest instance known of its
use in the signification referred to. Then
follows the second definition — "a native of
America of European descent, *esp.* a citizen of
the United States" — with other four quotations, dated respectively 1765, 1775, 1809 and
1882. The paragraph presents, as will be seen,
a complete history of the word, showing that
it began to be used toward the end of the sixteenth century; that it continued to bear its
original significance, as indicating one of the
savages encountered by the European discover-

ers and explorers of this continent, for about
two hundred years, after which time it came to
indicate a white settler, and was ultimately restricted, in common speech, to a resident of one
particular part of America, the United States.

The gratification, to any person who cares to
pursue even desultory and superficial study of
our language, of having such information as
this, so accurate, so full, so sententiously expressed — is unspeakable; but think of the labor
of compiling it! No one man, no ordinary association of men, could have made any considerable headway in an undertaking so colossal.
Only by the aid of hundreds of voluntary assis-
tants, all over the English-speaking world, working together energetically and persistently, could
the design have been executed. It is therefore
not surprising that more than a quarter of a
century elapsed between the time when the
proposal to compile such a dictionary was first
considered by the Philological Society (in 1857),
and the appearance of the first installment (in
1884). The work was not prosecuted syste-
matically and steadily during all this period,
however, the interest in accomplishing it, intense

at first, having wavered for a time and then
revived. When the present editor took charge,
in 1879, he found that " upwards of two million
quotations had been amassed," the paper slips
on which they were noted weighing, together
with correspondence and other necessary material, about two tons!   There was not nearly
enough, however; and Dr. Murray applied himself no less energetically to the task of getting
more readers at work than to that of putting in
order the accumulations already in hand.   The
assistance of some 1300 persons, examining the
works of more than 5000 authors, was ultimately
secured; and about 3,500,000 quotations had
been gathered (and arranged in preliminary
shape by thirty sub-editors) before the final
writing of the work was actually begun.   During
the last fifteen or twenty years, steady progress
has been made, and it would seem that the completion of the colossal undertaking might reason-
ably be expected early in the coming century.
The letters A, B and C, filling the first two volumes, are complete; so also is E, which will
constitute the last part of Vol. 3; portions of
D and of F have been issued; and G and H

are in active preparation. If the relative pro-
portions of this dictionary prove to be not unlike those of others, the completion of *H* will
leave not greatly more than half yet to be
published.

II.

IT will by this time have been perceived, if
not previously understood, that the question
which forms the second part of the title of this
chapter — a question very often asked of persons supposed to have paid special attention to
such matters — cannot be answered by naming
a single work. You might almost as well undertake to pick out the " best " magazine, the
" best " college, the " best " medicine. If by
" best " is understood the highest real excellence, there can be no question that for full
explanation of the history of our words in English, Murray is incomparably superior to any
other; but the inquirer may have, probably has,
some quite different kind of superiority in mind.
If it is the etymology of our words that he is
after, and their relationship with each other —
due weight being given to the important con-

siderations of clearness and brevity — Skeat[1] is decidedly the best; for matters of spelling and pronunciation, where of course there is room for difference of opinion, many good judges prefer respectively Worcester and perhaps on the whole Stormonth; for explanations of the things that words indicate, as well as the words themselves, one should select the Century, the Encyclopædic or the Standard; for general and hasty reference in everything, remembering that good and bad English is recognized in that work on about equal terms, Webster. Here are eight " bests" to choose from.

But as the question is commonly asked, it probably means something more like this: " What English dictionary is at the present day the best purchase for an American who does not intend seriously to study the language, but desires one such work, and one only, for the purpose of settling off-hand the questions on which one naturally goes to a dictionary as the

[1] A most admirable work, but not a *general* dictionary, being devoted entirely to etymology. It is published in two forms, the original quarto and the entirely re-written and re-arranged octavo — the latter being in some respects actually preferable to the former.

readiest source of information?" This modification puts Skeat and Murray out of court at
once. Indispensable to the philologist, they
would be very bad purchases to the general
reader; the first he would find utterly useless,
and while the second contains about all that he
might want, it contains also so much else that
he would be buying — from his point of view
— a bushel of chaff for a pint or so of grain.
Another admirable work, Worcester, it is also
unadvisable for anybody but a regular collector
of dictionaries now to buy, for reasons already
given; it is practically antiquated. If one
wants a cyclopædia and dictionary combined,
and does not object to paying $60, the Cen-
tury would be the natural choice. The Standard, at $12, is however relatively very much
cheaper; and the Americanized Encyclopædic,
costing only half that sum, though a larger
work, is much cheaper still — decidedly and
greatly the cheapest dictionary ever published,
though by no means a handsome work, and
to critical book-buyers rather unsatisfactory
from the very fact of its having been worked
over for the American market. If one wants

only a dictionary of words, without explanations of things, the latest and largest Stormonth, costing $6, should suit him perfectly. For a small dictionary for school use and similar purposes, one of the earlier editions of the same work is, on the whole, I think, preferable to any other. Here, as elsewhere, different men have different opinions, and for steady use the small type might be objectionable to some persons. But the book contains so much more matter than any other of the same size, and such excellent matter at that, as to present unique attractions; precious things are often done up in small parcels. Midway between the pure word-books and the cyclopædic compilations, stands the $10 International — a sort of happy compromise, and there is no denying that a certain interest will long attach, in this country, to knowing exactly what "Webster" says. It should be noted, finally, — as another point to perplex the chooser and the adviser — that the colored plates of the International and the Standard furnish full and accurate information on a number of subjects which are perhaps not often in question, but on which, when one does wish

to investigate them, it is extremely difficult to
find the facts clearly stated, outside of these
works.

III.

THREE curiosities of English lexicography
may be mentioned in closing. One is the repro-
duction, by several publishers, forty years after
its original appearance (the copyright having
meanwhile expired), of the Webster Unabridged
of 1847. It was photographed page by page,
and what are practically stereotype plates executed from the photographs, at a small fraction
of what would have been the cost of re-setting
in type. From these plates various editions,
exhibiting various degrees of bad printing, were
worked off, generally on miserable paper, and
with very flimsy binding, rendering it possible to
sell the work at a trifling sum, a dollar or less.
Thousands of copies must have been marketed,
the name "Webster Unabridged" being enough,
it seems, to float them. The transaction exhib-
its in strong light the immense popularity of
Webster's work. What other dictionary forty
years old would have a ghost of a chance of
finding itself thus resurrected?

The second curiosity to be mentioned is " The Progressive Dictionary," published by the Rev. Dr. Samuel Fallows in 1883, and described on the title-page as " a supplementary word-book to all the leading dictionaries of the United States and Great Britain, containing over forty thousand new words, definitions, and phrases.' It has between 500 and 600 pages, of about the size of those of the last Webster's Unabridged, and was sold for $5.

The third, perhaps most curious of all, is the " Dictionary of English Phrases," prepared by a full-blooded native of China, Mr. Kwong Ki Chiu, and published in 1881. This is really a dictionary of English words, though confined to such as are used in idiomatic expressions which have meanings that could not readily be ascertained from the ordinary definitions of their component words; and it is intended chiefly for the benefit of foreigners learning our language. As the introduction says: " ' To give ear,' in the literal sense, would mean something which requires no expression, since no such thing ever takes place; but the ear has been made to stand for the office or use which the ear was organized to serve, and the phrase, 'to give ear,' has been coined to express the idea of listening or giving one's attention." The book is an octavo of over nine hundred pages — containing, however, some appended matter about the history of China, with a sketch of the life of Christ, all which will be found interesting, and quite out of the ordinary run — to use a phrase that might well have claimed Mr. Kwong's attention, though he seems to have overlooked it. He did not overlook much, however; and while of course the book can have little or no practical value for persons to whom the knowledge of English came as a birthright, no collection of lexicons of our language is complete without it. The task of compiling such a work would be, one might think, just about the very last and most hopeless literary enterprise that it would ever enter the mind of a Chinaman to undertake.

AMERICAN ENGLISH.

And you may have a pretty considerable good sort of a feeble notion that it don't fit nohow; and that it ain't calculated to make you smart overmuch; and that you don't feel 'special bright, and by no means first-rate, and not at all tonguey; and that, however rowdy you may be by natur', it does use you up com-plete, and that's a fact; and makes you quake considerable, and disposed toe damn the engīne ! — All of which phrases, I beg to add, are pure Americanisms of the first water. — *Charles Dickens, Letter to John Forster.*

THE time-honored jokes about the "American language," if not entirely antiquated, have at least for the most part changed their longitude from the meridian of Greenwich. A recent attempt dates from the land of the Pharaohs. Riaz Pacha, late President of the Egyptian Council, is said to have retorted, on being rallied by an American for supporting so patiently the British yoke, that in one respect at least the English were making greater progress in the United States than in the East, inasmuch as he was credibly informed that their language was now almost universally spoken among the Americans! This is perhaps endurable; but it would subject one's politeness to a pretty severe strain, now-a-days, to be expected to appear greatly amused at a story about compliments paid in Great Britain to the good English spoken by some exceptional traveler from New York or Boston. Serious references, moreover, like that of Dean Alford, in his ridiculous book with a ridiculous title,[1] to "the process of deterioration" which the language "has undergone at the hands of the Americans," are not often found in British publications of recent date, except when accompanied (as was the dean's)[2] by some display of insular prejudice or crass ignorance in regard to the history, geography or politics of the

[1] "The Queen's English"—as if phrases like "the King's English," "the King's highway," the "King's evil," needed correction in gender when the sovereign happens to be a woman!

[2] "Look," he says, speaking of "the Americans," and writing in 1864, "at those phrases which so amuse us in their speech and books; . . . and then compare the character and history of the nation; . . . its reckless and fruitless maintenance of the most cruel and unprincipled war in the history of the world!"

United States, such as would naturally dis-
qualify the writer, in the mind of an impartial
judge, as a critic of anything pertaining to
this country. The testimony of well-informed
British writers of the present day is, in fact,
more generally in accord with that of Sir
George Campbell: "Of the body of the
[American] people it may be said that their
language is a little better than that used in
any county of England."[1]

Yet one does occasionally see, even in these
days, remarks in Dean Alford's tone in high-
class British periodicals. So late as Aug. 28,
1892, the fashionable Court Journal of London
informed its readers that "the inhabitants" of
the United States "have so far progressed with
their self-inflicted task of creating an American
language that much of their conversation is
incomprehensible to English people." A few
years earlier, the Westminster Review said,
editorially, that "the modifications which
differentiate 'American' from English are for
the most part vulgarisms, which, while they
heighten the effect of comic writing, are blots

[1] "White and Black," p. 23.

on more serious productions." Some months earlier still, but long after Alford's time, so important a periodical as the Nineteenth Century gave place to an article, by Dr. Fitzedward Hall, in which it was gravely, as well as elegantly, stated that William Cullen Bryant lived "among a people among whom our language is daily becoming more and more depraved," and that whoever compares the diction of "Edgar Huntly," an almost forgotten novel published in 1799, with Mr. Bryant's letters, "the English of which is not much worse than that of ninety-nine out of every hundred of his college-bred compatriots, will very soon become aware to what degree the art of writing our language has declined among educated" people in the United States!

The last quoted deliverance is perhaps the only one of the three that merits serious consideration, for the reason that Dr. Hall is a recognized authority in philology, whereas we know nothing as to the qualifications to discuss such matters that may or may not be possessed by the anonymous writers referred to. Dr. Hall's statement, if correct, is certainly alarming, and

we had better hearken to the words of reproof
and mend our ways before the mother tongue,
depraved beyond hope by our evil communi-
cations, declines in this country into utter
worthlessness. Two considerations, nevertheless, may afford a ray of hope that the case
is not altogether desperate. One is, that our
censor is — not a Briton, as might be supposed,
but one of those extraordinary Americans of
the "Carroll Gansevoort"[1] stripe who seem to
regard it rather as matter of regret than otherwise that they were not born in Europe, and
who commonly out-British the British themselves in reviling the customs of the United
States; it is just possible, therefore, that his
judgment may not be absolutely impartial and

---

[1] In Edgar Fawcett's bright story, "A Gentleman of Leisure," Mr. Gansevoort, a New Yorker by birth, who "would
have considered himself disgraced if he wore a pair of trousers
or carried an umbrella that was not of English make,"
rebukes a friend for committing the frightful Americanism
of saying that he fished with a pole (instead of a rod), and
on the culprit's perpetrating the further enormity of speaking of catching four dozen fine trout, remarks : "Upon
my word, I beg your pardon, old fellow, but it always amuses
them so on the other side when we speak about *catching* fish.
There they don't catch them, you know ; they kill them !"

unprejudiced. The other hopeful consideration is that the historian Prescott, tolerably
good authority on the use of English, regarded
the style of the author of "Edgar Huntly" as
characterized by "unnatural condensation,
unusual and pedantic epithets and elliptical
forms of expression, *in perpetual violation of
idiom;*" it is just possible, therefore, that Dr.
Hall, with all his acquirements in scientific
linguistics, may not know quite as much as he
supposes he does about the correct use of our
(more or less) Anglo-Saxon vernacular.

At the same time, the occasional appearance in England of an article like those from
which are taken the elegant extracts in the last
paragraph but one, is a phenomenon which
suggests two interesting reflections. The first,
of comparatively minor importance, is merely
that some of our English cousins have a good
deal yet to learn about our common language
as used in the two countries. The second is,
that where there is so much smoke there must
be some flame.   That is, making all allow-
ances, there must really exist certain noticeable
variations between the styles of writing and

speaking that are current on the opposite sides of the Atlantic; for if no differences at all could be found, it is hardly probable that any intelligent man, however strongly British his prepossessions, would care to publish a dissertation in which our practice is deliberately set down as distinctly inferior to that of his own nation. In what these differences consist, and in what particulars the mother tongue may be thought to have become especially "depraved" in this country, are questions deserving attention.

I.

In the first place, it will hardly be denied in any quarter that the speech of the United States is quite unlike that of Great Britain in the important particular that *we have no dialects.* "I never found any difficulty in understanding an American speaker," writes the historian Freeman;[1] "but I have often found it

[1] Article, "Some Impressions of the United States," published in the Fortnightly Review, and copied into the Eclectic for October, 1882, p. 435, and Littell for September 9, 1882, No. 1994, p. 602.

difficult to understand a Northern-English speaker." "From Portland, Me., to Portland, Oregon," says a writer in the Westminster Review (July, 1888, p. 35), "no trace of a distinct dialect is to be found. The man from Maine, even though he may be of inferior education and limited capacity, can completely understand the man of Oregon. There is no peasant with a *patois* ; there is no rough Northumbrian burr; in point of fact, there is no brogue." Trifling variations in pronunciation, and in the use of a few particular words, certainly exist. The Yankee "expects" or "calculates," while the Virginian "reckons; " the illiterate Northerner "claims,"[1] and the Southerner of similar class, by a very curious reversal of the blunder, "allows," what better educated people merely assert. The pails and pans of the world at large become "buckets " when taken to Kentucky. It is "evening" in

[1] And sometimes, alas ! the Northerner who is not illiterate. Prof. Whitney, editor of the great Century Dictionary, is more than once guilty of this solecism in his " Elements of English Pronunciation; " and so is Prof. L. T. Townsend of the Boston University, in his work on the "Art of Speech," published by the Appletons in 1881.

Richmond while afternoon still lingers a hundred miles due north at Washington. Vessels go into "docks" on their arrival at Philadelphia, but into "slips" at Mobile; they are tied up to "wharves" at Boston, but to "piers" at Milwaukee. Distances from place to place are measured by "squares" in Baltimore, by "blocks" in Chicago. The "shilling" of New York is the "levy" of Pennsylvania, the "bit" of San Francisco, the "ninepence" of old New England, and the "escalan" of New Orleans. But put all these variations together, with such others as more microscopic examination might reveal, and how far short they fall of representing anything like the real dialectic differences of speech that obtain, and always have obtained, not only as between the three kingdoms, but even between contiguous sections of England itself! What great city of this country, for example, has developed, or is likely to develop, any peculiar class of errors at all comparable in importance to those of the cockney speech of London? What two regions can be found within our borders, however sequestered and unenlightened, and however

widely separated by geographical position, of
which the speech of the one presents any
difficulty worth mentioning, or even any very
startling unfamiliarity in sound or construction,
to the inhabitant of the other? Our omnipre-
sent railroads, telegraph lines, mail routes and
printing presses, and the well-marked disposi-
tion of every class of our people to make
lavish use of these means of intercommunica-
tion, both for the rapid diffusion of intelligence
and the interchange of opinion, and also, so
far as lines of travel are concerned, for the
frequent transportation of the people themselves hither and thither, with a degree of ease
and celerity to which no other country has
ever attained — these causes have always fa-
vored, and seem likely permanently to preserve,
a certain community of expression as well as
of thought, that is not only practically prohibi-
tive of the formation of new dialects, but also
rapidly effaces the prominent lineaments of
such variations as have at different times been
imported from the old world. If then, in this
particular respect, we are depraving our mother
tongue, the only logical inference that can be

drawn is that a language reaches its best estate in proportion as it is diversified by local peculiarities.

It ought to be remembered also, in this immediate connection, that the ordinary speech of the United States presents not greatly more of what may be called caste variations than of those that are attributable to differences of locality. A discriminating English traveler, the Rev. F. Barham Zincke, Vicar of Wherstead and Chaplain-in-Ordinary to the Queen, has mentioned as "a remarkable fact that the English spoken in America is not only very pure, but also is spoken with equal purity by all classes. * * The language in every man's mouth," he adds, "is that of literature and society. * * It is even the language of the negroes of the towns." [1] In other words, the speech of the lower orders of our people, even down to the very substrata, whether examined in regard to its vocabulary, its construction or its pronunciation, differs from what all admit to be standard correctness in a much smaller

[1] "Last Winter in the United States;" John Murray, London, 1863.

degree than we have every reason to believe
to be the case in England, our enemies themselves being judges.   A careful comparison
of slang dictionaries, I think, will reveal a far
longer list of unauthorized words as current
among British thieves and "cadgers" than
among their congeners in the United States.
Grammatical rules are violated badly enough
by the ignorant of our own cities every day,
no doubt; but how often, after all, will you
hear from intelligent and respectable working
people of American descent quite such a solecism as the "I were" and "he were" that are so
frequently noticed in the mouths of lower-
middle-class Britons, accustomed all their lives
to conversation with speakers of the purest
English?   And as for pronunciation, we have
our faults, of course, in abundance, the best of
us as well as the most careless, and should
amend them with all diligence; but where,
from the Atlantic to the Pacific, will you discover any such utter disability of hearing or
discernment as can permit men to drop or
multiply their *h's* or transpose their *w's* and
v's?

II.

Speaking of pronunciation, and with regard to the sound of the language as used by the educated people of the two countries (a point which most writers on Americanisms pass over with the briefest notice, though one of the ablest of them all, Prof. George P. Marsh, has devoted to it his chief attention), it must be admitted, I think, that if the typical English intonation is better than ours, it is because the office of language is what Talleyrand said it was — to conceal one's thought. That is to say, the average American college graduate, for instance, will speak more intelligibly and more agreeably wherever there is any difficulty in speaking, as before a large assembly or in the open air, than will the English university man. The Yankee may talk through his nose, to be sure; may unduly emphasize minor words, cut off terminal letters rather abruptly, or select too high a key; but he will not say *readin'*, *writin'*, *speakin'*; he will not gulp or sputter; he will seldom insert superfluous *aw's* or *ugh's*, and the reporter who may have to follow his utterance will be far less liable to lose parts of a sentence, or to mistake one phrase for another, than in discharging the same duty on the other side.

And when it comes to orthoëpy proper, the deliberate sounding of single words, it will be found that in almost every case the difference is due to the American's following more closely than does the Briton the spelling of the word — a practice which can hardly result in depraving the language, but seems rather to suggest that the American is the greater reader of the two, and therefore likely to be the safer guide in questions of verbal correctness. Thus the now thoroughly anglicized French word *trait*, in which none of us ever thinks of dropping the final *t*, is still commonly called *tray* in England, and that pronunciation is given the place of honor in the best British authority, Stormonth's excellent dictionary. The *l* of *almond*, commonly sounded in this country, is silent abroad. *Sliver*, which Americans call *slīver*, following the obvious analogy of the more common word *liver*, and following, too, the example of the poet Chaucer, is largely called *sliver* in Great Britain. *Schedule*, which we invariably pronounce *skedule*, constitutes in England almost the only exception to the rule that *ch* is hard after initial *s*, being there called *shedule* or *sedule*. The verb *to perfect*, invariably pronounced like the adjective in England, with accent on the first syllable, is very often heard as per*fect'* in this country, thus bringing it into harmony with *perfume, cement, desert, present, produce, progress, project, rebel, record* and other words which are accented on the final syllable when used as verbs, but not otherwise. *Nephew* and *phial*, which constitute in England the only exceptions to the almost universal law that the digraph *ph*, when sounded at all, is sounded like *f*, are both reduced to rule in this country, by pronouncing the first *nefew* and spelling the second *vial*. *Hostler*, always pronounced in this country as it is spelled, is marked *'ostler* in Stormonth.

And in respect to geographical names, the closer adherence of our countrymen to the guidance of the orthography is, of course, notorious and manifest. Except the dropping, in imitation of the French, of the final *s* of *Illinois;* the two words *Connecticut* and *Arkansas* (the latter a very doubtful exception); and a few terms like *Sioux*, derived from corruptions of Indian names — it is not easy to recall any geographical appellation indigenous to our soil which is not pronounced very nearly as it is spelled. And when names are imported with a well-authorized divergence between the sound and the spelling, a strong tendency toward the obliteration of this divergence is sure to become manifest. *Warwick* is about as often *Warwick* as *War'ick* when spoken of in America; *Norwich* is more commonly *Norwich*, I think, than *Noridge ; St. Louis* and *Louisville* are often called *St. Lewis* and *Lewisville ;* a resident of Delaware County in New York would not know what place was meant if you spoke of the county seat as "Daily," so perfectly settled is "Delhi" as the pronunciation as well as the spelling of the name. A multitude of other instances might be mentioned, among the most remarkable of which, perhaps, is the change that has taken place in the popular sounding of the name

Chautauqua. As long as it was spelled with a
final *e*, people persisted in saying *Chautawk,*
notwithstanding that the local practice was
always otherwise; but an immediate reformation was effected, some thirty years ago, by
the simple expedient of substituting an *a*. It
is probably quite safe to say that no mispro-
nunciation of a geographical name, growing
out of an attempt to follow too closely the
sound of its letters, has ever become so prevalent in Great Britain as even to suggest the
idea of making the spelling conform to the
orthoëpy, and, furthermore, that if such a
difficulty ocurred, the attempted remedy in
question would be found in that country quite
unproductive of any change in the popular
usage.

III.

Passing from orthoëpy to orthography, it
hardly need be said that in every instance
without exception where a change in spelling
has originated in the United States, the change
has been in the direction of simplicity, and in
the interest therefore of the " reform " which

the Philological Society of Great Britain (not
to mention such individual names as Max
Müller, Dr. J. A. H. Murray, Prof. Newman,
the Duke of Richmond, and Mr. Gladstone)
so warmly favors. The dropping of the second
g in *waggon*, the *u* in *parlour* and similar
words, the *me* in *programme* (who would think
of writting *diagramme* or *telegramme?*), the
e in *storey* (of a house), and the final *e* in *pease*[1]
(plural of pea), are all changes in this direction; and so is the substitution of *w* for *ugh* in
plough, and *f* for *ugh* in *draught*, and the aban-
donment of the spellings *cheque, shew, cyder,*[2]
and especially *gaol*, the universal adoption of
jail bringing this word into harmony with the
rest of the language, as there is no other instance in English of a soft *g* before *a* — notwithstanding that some absurd people, who do
not call Margaret *Marjaret* or Garfield *Jarfield*,
will persist in saying *oleomarjarine.*

It should be noted, moreover, that our
American practice of dropping the *u* from

[1] Of course *pease* was not originally a plural word, but nobody thinks of it otherwise now.

[2] See Halliwell's Dictionary, art. " Griggles."

many words formerly ending in *our* is more than a movement in the direction of spelling reform, for it cancels the etymological misinformation suggested by the old-fashioned orthography not yet extinct in England. Some people imagine that the *u* in these words has value, or at least a certain sort of interest, as indicating that they came to us through the French and not directly from Latin or from other tongues, — rather an unimportant matter at best; but the trouble is that, with the exception perhaps of one single word, *savour*, the indication either points the wrong way or would almost certainly be overlooked except by persons familiar with entirely obsolete spellings in French. The *u* is omitted, even in England, from *governor*, *emperor*, *senator*, *error*, *ancestor*, *ambassador*, *progenitor*, *successor*, *metaphor*, *bachelor*, *exterior*, *inferior* and *superior*, every one of which is of French origin, while it is used in *neighbor*, *flavor*, *harbor* and *arbor*, which are not French. Even in *honor*, *favor*, *labor*, *armor*, *odor*, *vapor*, *savior* and *parlor*, where the *u* has some color of right to be found, it is doubtful whether its insertion has value as suggesting

French derivation, for in the case of the first six of these words the ordinary reader would be quite certain to have in mind only the modern spellings — *honneur, faveur, labeur, armure, odeur* and *vapeur* — which have the *u* indeed, but no *o;* while *savior* and *parlor* come from old French words that are themselves without the *u* — *saveor* and *parleor.* The *u* in all these words is therefore either useless or positively misleading. And finally, in the case of *color, humor* and *valor,* it is to be remarked that the exact American orthography actually occurs in old French.

IV.

In respect to at least one Yankee spelling, . that of *plow,* and probably others, it should not be forgotten that the prevalent practice in this country agrees with the universal custom of an earlier time, from which divergence without good reason has gradually grown up in England. ˙ And this brings us to another strongly marked characteristic of our American speech — its greater permanence and steadiness, so to speak, as compared with that of the mother country.

This peculiarity will appear very clearly, where it might least be expected, on close examination of any list of words supposed to have been greatly distorted in their meaning, or even manufactured out of whole cloth, by erring Yankees, a very large proportion of which will almost always be found to be good old English, grown obsolescent or obsolete at home, but preserved in the New World in their pristine vitality and force; and conversely, on examining such a book as Halliwell's Dictionary of Archaisms and Provincialisms, which contains, presumably, no word now in good use in Great Britain in the meaning given, the American reader will discover a great number of terms — nearly three hundred, I should say — with which he is perfectly familiar. I give a few examples, not including any that are marked as provincial, the implication being that all these words were once good English, but are no longer in common use in the mother country:

Adze (a carpenter's tool); *affectation* ("a curious desire for a thing which nature hath not given"); *afterclap; agape; age* as a verb; *air* in the sense of appearance; *amerce; andi·*

rons ; angry, said of a wound; *appellant* (one who appeals); *apple-pie order ; baker's dozen ; bamboozle ; bay* in a barn; *bay* window; *bearers* at a funeral; *berate ; between whiles ; bicker ; blanch* (to whiten); *brain* as a verb; *burly ; cast* (to tie and throw down, as a horse); *catcall ; cesspool ; chafe* (to grow angry); *clodhopper ; clutch* (to seize); *clutter ; cockerel ; coddle ; copious ; cosey ; counterfeit* money; *crazy* in the sense of dilapidated, as applied to a building; *crock* (an earthen vessel); *crone* (an old woman); *crook* (a bend); *croon ; cross-grained* in the sense of obstinate or peevish; *cross-patch ; cross purposes ; cuddle ; cuff* (to beat); *deft ; din ; dormer* window; *earnest,* money given to bind a bargain; *egg on ; greenhorn ; hasp ; jack of all trades ; jamb* of a door; *lintel ; list* (selvage of cloth); *loop* hole; *nettled* (out of temper); *newel ; ornate ; perforce ; piping hot ; pit* (mark left by small-pox); *quail* (to shrink); *ragamuffin ; riffraff ; rigmarole ; scant ; seedy* ("miserable looking"); *shingles ; sorrel* (the color); *out of sorts ; stale* ("wanting freshness"); *sutler ; thill ; toady ; trash ; underpinning.* All these words, with many others equally familiar in the

United States, are apparently regarded by Halliwell as having become obsolete in England.

It would not be difficult, on the other hand, to compile quite a list of Briticisms, including words recently invented in Great Britain (where the "boldness of innovation on this subject," amounting to "absolute licentiousness," which Noah Webster notes and deplores in his preface of 1847, still runs rampant) — such as *totalling*, or (still worse) *totting*, for adding up; *navvy*, for laborer; *fad*, for hobby; *randomly*, for at random; *outing*, for pleasure excursion; *tund*, for beat[1]; *bumper*, for enormous[2]; *picked* for aborted[3] ; and a larger class of old words now used in that country in a comparatively new and in some respects objectionable signification not generally recognized in the United States.

I remember hearing with astonishment, some twenty years ago, from an English gentleman of

---

[1] Even Spencer condescends to the use of this extraordinary vocable, though he offers a sort of semi-apology by putting it in quotation marks. — *Study of Sociology*, chap. 8.

[2] "The *bumper* wheat crop now expected by American agriculturists." — *Editorial in Mark Lane Express, June* 1, 1891.

[3] "Mr. Buchanan's mare Maggie has *picked* twin foals." — *North British Agriculturist, April* 30, 1890.

culture and high social standing, that it was necessary to remove the gates of Quebec, " to give more room for *traffic.*" I asked no questions, but wondered inwardly whether the people of the American Gibraltar were in the habit, like the ancient Orientals, of resorting to the gates of the town to exchange commodities with each other. On our arrival next morning, the mystery was solved; it was travel, not barter, that my friend meant by traffic. The word is continually thus misused in England, and it must be sorrowfully admitted that the bad habit is now invading this country as well, not so much among the people, however, as in a kind of technical way. The New-York Central Railroad, for instance, has a " general traffic manager," who certainly manages no traffic, the corporation being carriers and not traders.

Other examples — as yet, happily, not naturalized in American usage — are: *Knockcd-up,* for fatigued; *Famous* for excellent — " we have had a famous walk," meaning an enjoyable one; *bargain,* for haggle [1] — " Mr. Boffin, I never

[1] The anonymous author of Chatto and Windus' Slang Dictionary (new edition, London, 1874) falls into this error,

bargain," says Silas Wegg in Our Mutual Friend
(book I, chap. 5) — he was bargaining at that
very moment; *tiresome*, for disagreeable; the
particularly refined and elegant expression *rot*,
for nonsense; *jug*, for pitcher; *good form*, for in
good taste; *trap*, for carriage; *tub*, for bathe; to
wire, for to telegraph; *starved*, for frozen; *stop*, —
for stay — " no paint will stop on them," says
the heroine of Wilkie Collins' " No Name; " *as-* —
sist, for be present, as the silent auditors at a
concert are absurdly said to " assist " at it;
plant for fixtures, as the " plant " of a railway or
a factory; *intimate*, for announce — advertisers
in British newspapers continually " intimate " to
their customers that they have changed their
their quarters or received new goods; *caucus* —
" grotesquely misapplied " in England, says the
highest British authority, Murray's Philological
Dictionary, " to an organization or system " ;
and *tidy*, for almost anything complimentary —
a London paper made mention the other day of
" a very tidy bull," the writer meaning a valuable animal, and by no means intending to

which surely ought not to be expected of a lexicographer.
See page 353 of the work referred to.

refer to any particular cleanliness in the beast's personal habits. English hostlers also — to get pretty well down in the social scale, though by no means going as low as do the compilers of what are termed Americanisms, in their search for blunders — English hostlers sometimes speak of *chilling* cold water, meaning warming it, an extraordinary perversion of a very common and elementary word.

It is not only, however, in their recent coinages and anomalous assigning of new meanings to old terms, that the English have made reckless changes in the body of our speech where the American practice adheres to the former standard. They have swung off in the opposite direction also, curtailing to no good purpose the significance of several words. A "young person," is always a girl in England, the term being never applied to a boy. An invalid is "ill," not sick, unless he happens to be nauseated, while at the same time, strangely enough, it is regarded as perfectly proper to describe him as confined to a sick-room or stretched upon a sick-bed, and the English prayer-book not only contains services for the "visitation of the sick" and the " communion of the sick," but requires those who use it to make intercession for " all sick persons " as often as the Litany is read. A latter-day Briton — notwithstanding an example so recent as Macaulay, " the richest inhabitants exhibited their wealth, not by riding in carriages " — is horrified at the idea of *riding* in anything built on the coach plan, though he makes no scruple of riding in an omnibus or a street-car; when you enter the vehicle at the side, you drive; when at the end, you ride. A *beast*, moreover, is now in Great Britain a member of the genus *bos*, and almost always an animal that is to be fed for beef, at that; English official market reports give prices for " beasts," " sheep," " calves," " pigs," and " milch cows "; and I read not long ago in a Dublin newspaper, speaking of rabies, that " two dogs, five *beasts*, one pig and one horse were killed during the week." If the author of " Macleod of Dare " is a trustworthy guide, the word *up*, used in reference to a journey in Great Britain, indicates, not that the traveller is seeking a more elevated region or moving northwardly, but solely that he is going toward the capital; " up to London " and " down to the Highlands" are, it appears, the correct formulæ. No wonder the young Scotchman thought it sounded " stupid." Fancy a man in Chicago saying that he was going "up to Washington," or a man in Washington speaking of events occurring "down in St. Paul!"

A third kind of variation that seems to have grown up in Great Britain to a greater degree than in this country, is the habit of turning active and especially reflexive verbs into neuters by dropping the object, as, " Don't trouble " for "Don't trouble yourself." [1]   It is true that a tendency in this direction can be traced a long way back in the history of the language. To *repent*, to *endeavor*, and some other now neuter verbs, were formerly reflexives; one *endeavored himself* in the same sense that we now *apply ourselves*, and *repented himself* as we now *bethink ourselves*.   It is also true that a few alterations of this kind not yet sanctioned by good usage, but occasionally heard, may be said properly enough to be common to the two countries; " I avail of this opportunity," for " I avail myself of

[1] " We do not trouble to inquire." — *London Law Times*, quoted in *Albany Law Journal*, vol. 26, p. 121.

this opportunity," is one.   But I think any careful reader of the now current literature of
England and the United States will approve
the opinion that our British brethren are going
much faster in this direction than are we.   As
long ago as 1854 Miss Yonge wrote (in Hearts-
ease, part II, chapter 10): "Theodora flung
away and was rushing off."   Charles Reade,
whom the astute Fitzedward Hall ranks among
" the choicest of living English writers,"[1] is
guilty of such phrases as "Wardlaw whipped
before him " (Foul Play, chap. 15), "Ransome
whipped before it" (Put Yourself in his Place,
chapter 31), [Little] "flung out of the room "
(same, chapter 32), and various others.   These
and similar incomplete sentences, not at all
uncommon in British books and periodicals,
certainly strike the American ear as decided
innovations, and constitute a peculiarity of diction very rarely to be observed on this side of
the water.

The English have also a practice, more pronounced by far than our own, of abbreviating a
good many words in their common talk.   They

---

[1] Scribner's Monthly, vol. 3, p. 701.

never call their consolidated government bonds anything but "consols," or the process of hypothecation anything but "hypothec." The Zoölogical Gardens in London are commonly known as the "Zoo," and a series of delightful popular concerts given every season in the same city are euphoniously denominated the "Monday pops." Hampshire, not in writing only, but in speech as well, is "Hants," Buckinghamshire is "Bucks," and Hertfordshire "Herts." A public house is a "public." A similar liberty is taken with the names of firms; "Smith & Co." is often made to do duty, even in formal business letters, for the established title, "Smith, Brown & Robinson." One well known American publishing house, Messrs. Ticknor & Fields of Boston, did at one time imitate this form of contraction, by gilding "Ticknor & Co." on the backs of their books; but the practice has been abandoned by their successors, and I do not know that any other American house ever followed the example. Certain it is that about the longest and most awkward name in the book trade "Cassell, Petter, Galpin & Co.," was always written in full in this country, though often contracted (be-

fore it was changed) into Cassell & Co., in
England.

In the construction of many sentences, however, an opposite plan is frequently followed —
the insertion of utterly superfluous words. So
important a writer as Henry J. Nicoll says —
" Landmarks of English Literature," introduction, p. 18 — " Every critic occasionally meets
in with works of great fame of which he cannot
appreciate the merit." Beaconsfield writes —
" Endymion," chap. 100: " He was *by way of*
intimating that he was engaged in a great
work." So a writer in Cassell's Magazine, Feb-
ruary, 1893, p. 123: " She was *by way of* painting the shrimp girl." In Herbert Spencer's
Treatise on Education, chap. 10, we read that " in
Russia the infant mortality is *something* enormous," and in one of Charles Dickens' letters to
Mr. Forster: " The daily difference in [a ship's]
rolling, as she burns the coals out, is *something*
absolutely fearful." [1] It hardly need be remarked that the italicized words in all these
sentences have to be removed before they be-

[1] " A Short Life of Charles Dickens," Appletons' Handy
Volume Series, p. 116.

come intelligible, or at least agreeable to persons appreciating really correct speech. The peculiar misuse of the affix *ever*, as in saying "what*ever* are you doing?" that one so often notices in the conversation particularly of English ladies, is another instance of the same failing; and who has not been annoyed and disgusted by the innumerable *got's* with which so many English pages fairly bristle? Three good illustrations occur in a single article, "A Few Words about the Nineteenth Century," by Frederic Harrison, in the Fortnightly Review: "He extolled him for possessing all the good qualities which he had not *got ;*" "for twenty thousand years man has *got* no better light than what was given by pitch, tallow or oil;" "I don't say but what this work has *got* to be done." Or glance over Endymion: "He has *got* a champion" (chap. 35); "I have *got* some House of Commons men dining with me" (chap. 50); "I have *got* a horse which I should like you to ride" (chap. 52); "Lady Montford maintained they had *got* nothing" (*id.*); "All you have *got* to do is to make up your mind" (chap. 65); "You have *got* a great deal of private business

to attend to " (chap. 99). So the Marquis of
Blandford, in the North American Review:
" The Irish members are a feature which we
have not at present *got* to deal with; " Spencer
in the book above referred to (Education, chap.
3): " Must not the child judge by such evidence
as he has *got ?* "   George Augustus Sala, Illustrated London News: " To my shame, I have
not *got* a Cowden-Clarke's concordance; " Wilkie Collins, Man and Wife, chap. 9: " I have
got a letter for you; " and in Marion Fay, chap.
3: " ' He has *got* money; ' ' but he is not therefore to be a tyrant; ' ' Yes, he is, over a daughter who has *got* none; ' " Charles Reade, Foul
Play, chap. 19: " I have *got* something for
you " — in none of which cases is the idea of
getting intended in the slightest degree to be
implied, but only that of present possession.
The general American dislike of this ugly word,
and our practice, where the past participle of the
verb *get* must be used, of adopting the old and
softer form *gotten* (which is now scarcely ever
used in England) [1] are not exactly what would

[1] See "English and American English," by R. A. Proctor,
in the Gentleman's Magazine, copied into Appletons' Journal

184 Our Common Speech.

be expected of a people who are ruining the language.

V.

I think moreover, though the opinion is of course only an opinion, and hardly susceptible of positive proof or absolute negation, that good English authors in general are less particular about many points of grammar than are Americans of the same class. Dean Alford is authority for the statement that "our best writers [meaning the best British writers] have the popular expression *these kind, those sort*,"[1] where *this kind* or *that sort* is intended; and I have noticed intances of this solecism in Bagehot (Physics and Politics, No. II, section 3 — "Nations with *these sort* of maxims") and in Miss Muloch (Agatha's Husband, chap. 1 — "The Iansons were *those sort* of religious people who think any Biblical allusions irreverent.") In a story called "The Ladies Lindores," published serially in Blackwood (part II, chap. 4, No.

for October, 1881, and the New York Tribune of Aug. 14, 1881.

[1] The Queen's English, 11th thousand, ¶ 98.

799 of the magazine,) we find the following:
"There are some happy writers whose mission
it is to expound the manners and customs of
the great. * * And yet, alas! to these writers
when they have done all, yet must we add that
they fail to satisfy their models. * * 'As if
these sort of people knew anything about
society!' Lady Adeliza says." Lady Adeliza,
or her reporter, would do well to study a certain
very elementary rule of grammar.

A writer in the Gentleman's Magazine, Mr.
Dudley Errington (see Littell's Living Age, No.
2038, p. 95), makes the following statement, referring to Great Britain only: "The fact is that
bade and *durst*, and even *dares*, have become all
but obsolete in our day, without any possible
reason either in grammar or in euphony. Why,
for instance, should not *bade* or *bidden* be used
in the following instances from the *Times* and
the *Quarterly Review?* 'Mr. Charles Dickens
finally *bid* farewell to Philadelphia.' — *Times.*
'Uncertain even at that epoch (1864) of Aus-
tria's fidelity, Prussia *bid* high for German
leadership.' — *Times.* 'He called his servants
and *bid* them procure firearms.' — *Times.* 'The

competition is so sharp and general that the leader of to-day can never be sure that he will not be *outbid* to-morrow.' — *Quarterly Review.* And why not *durst* in the following extract from the Rev. Charles Kingsley? 'Neither her maidens nor the priest *dare* speak to her for half an hour.' — '*Hereward the Wake.*'"

In the third series of Freeman's historical essays we find gems like the following: "One *whom* the mockers of the age said was no fitting guest;" " It may be argued that if he either could not *nor* would not hold Athens; " " The valiant peasantry of old Hellas was of another mould *from* the nobles;" and "Their relation to the empire was wholly different *to* that of the Illyrian slaves."

Worse than most of these slips is Charles Reade's not infrequent blundering with the nominative and objective cases, as where he makes the highborn and elegant Edward Fountain, Esq., of Font Abbey, inform his niece that "there will be only *us* two at dinner!" (Love me Little, Love me Long, chap. 1.) Worse still is the confusing of the verbs *lie* and lay, an error very rarely to be observed in respectable

American society, but one to which Alford says
Eton graduates are especially prone, and one
into which Anthony Trollope fell when he made
Mr. Harding (in "The Warden," chap. 7)
say: "I have done more than sleep upon it;
I have *laid* awake upon it." A striking instance of the occurrence of this confusion may
be found in an extraordinary place for a grammatical error, Stormonth's English Word-Book,
where *laid* is actually given as the participle of
lie! After noting this, one need hardly be surprised to find the same writer defining *Alborak*
(in the supplement to his dictionary) as "the
white mule on which Mohammed is said *to have
rode* from Jerusalem to heaven!" If an American lexicographer were caught using *laid* for
lain, or *rode* for *ridden*, what a text it would
furnish for a dissertation on the process of depraving our mother tongue which is advancing
with such alarming rapidity in the United
States!

About as bad as this, perhaps, is the remarkable phrase "*a good few*" that one sometimes
sees in very respectable British publications —
not exactly ungrammatical, of course, but funny,

so to speak. A British practice that manifestly *is* ungrammatical, and so extremely ungrammatical as to evince ignorance or disregard of one of the simplest principles of the structure of our language, is exemplified in such phrases as "an invention*s* exhibition," "the river*s* pollution commission" and the like. Nobody speaks of a hat*s* rack, or a book*s* case or a cloak*s* room, and everybody ought to know that a noun used to qualify another noun is for the time an adjective *and therefore absolutely indeclinable ;* but while this is perfectly recognized in England in the case of every *old* combination, it is repeatedly overlooked in making new ones — and overlooked in the most formal official documents even more than in the careless language of the newspapers, where it would be perhaps more pardonable.

Then there are certain highly incorrect constructions, like "different to," and "frightened of," which are notoriously British, and of which it is almost safe to say that no American is ever guilty. Spencer's "immediately this is recognized" (Study of Sociology, chap. 2), meaning *as soon as this is recognized*, and Buckle's

" directly they came" (letter to Mrs. Grey, quoted in Huth's Life, chap. 2) meaning *directly after they had come*, are other instances. Buckle, it should be remembered, was anything but a careless writer, having devoted great labor for a long time to the acquisition of a correct and polished style of composition. One would think he need not have spent many hours in this sort of study before discovering that such a sentence as "I put them away directly they came" is not English. (Since writing the last sentence, I have noticed, with sorrow, an instance of exactly the same error in one of G. W. Smalley's letters from London to the New York Tribune: "Directly he heard of the intended demonstration, Mr. Parnell left the train." But Mr. Smalley, like the lady in "The Mighty Dollar," has " lived so much abroad, you know," that some absorption of British blunders might well be expected of him; and I think one might spend a good deal of time in searching American literature, periodical or book, before he would find another case.)

Dr. Fitzedward Hall, as already quoted, is of opinion that educated people in this country have lost the ability to write our language as did the author of "Edgar Huntly" at the close of the last century. But what must he think of the improvement that has been made on the other side of the sea when he turns the pages of Endymion and notices the following, among other phrases of similar correctness and beauty? "*Everybody* says what *they* like" (chap. 20); "I would never leave him for a moment, *only* I know he would get wearied of me" (chap. 39); "I have never *been* back *to* the old place" (chap. 63); "*Everybody* can do exactly what *they* like" (chap. 98). Speaking in all seriousness, were it not on the whole preferable that the art of writing English should decline everywhere even faster than it has declined in this country, rather than that it should develop into such perfection as is illustrated by the last literary production of an ex-prime-minister of Great Britain?

VI.

Of course nobody thinks of denying, nevertheless, that a number of new, and in many cases uncalled-for, words and expressions have been invented and now pass current in the United States, or that the meaning of some others has been gradually warped, to the injury of the language, just as has occurred in England. This part of the subject has been laboriously investigated by several diligent students — so laboriously that there is little left to say about it except in the way of correction. Not to speak of articles in periodicals, brief essays, and single chapters, no fewer than seven books devoted entirely to so-called Americanisms in speech have from time to time appeared — Pickering's Vocabulary, in 1816; Noah Webster's " Letter," in 1817; Elwyn's Glossary, in 1859; Schele de Vere's Americanisms, in 1872; Bartlett's Dictionary, — the first edition in 1848, the second in 1859, the third in 1860, the fourth, considerably enlarged, in 1877; Farmer's Americanisms, in 1889; and Norton's Political Americanisms, in 1890. The student of language will find much to interest, and not a little to amuse him, in each of these collections of monstrosities.

VII.

JOHN PICKERING'S "VOCABULARY, OR COL-
LECTION OF WORDS AND PHRASES which have
been supposed to be peculiar to the United
States," originated in the author's practice,
while living in London during the first two
years of this century, of noting down, for the
purpose of avoiding them, such of his own
verbal expressions as were condemned for
American errors by his British friends. After
returning to this country, he communicated a
paper on the subject, consisting of an essay and
a list of words, to the American Academy of
Arts and Sciences, and shortly after, having
largely amplified the vocabulary, submitted the
whole to the candor of his countrymen for their
instruction and admonition. The poor man was
deeply concerned for the future of the language
in America, and very much in earnest in his
work. It might indeed be a long time, he
thought, before it should " be the lot of many
Americans to publish works which will be read
out of their own country; yet all who have the

least tincture of learning will continue to feel an ardent desire to acquaint themselves with English authors. Let us then," he proceeds, "imagine the time to have arrived when Americans shall no longer be able to understand the works of Milton, Pope, Swift, Addison and other English authors justly styled classic without the aid of a translation into a language that is to be called at some future day the American tongue! * * * Nor is this the only view in which a radical change of language would be an evil. To say nothing of the facilities afforded by a common language in the ordinary intercourse of business, it should not be forgotten that our religion and our laws are studied in the language of the nation from which we are descended; and, with the loss of the language, we should finally suffer the loss of those peculiar advantages which we now derive from the investigations of the jurists and divines of that country."

To do what lay in his power to avert a calamity so appalling, was the object that Mr. Pickering had in view; and lest his own impressions should be faulty, or his imperfect knowledge of pure English should prove inadequate to the

13

task of properly branding all the principal American corruptions, he took the pains of submitting his list to several well-informed friends, and particularly to two English gentle-men whose authority he considered beyond question, although he admits that as they had lived some twenty years in America, "their ear had lost much of that sensibility to deviations from the pure English idiom which would once have enabled them to pronounce with decision in cases where they now felt doubts." As finally published, the Vocabulary contains over five hundred words, of which not more than about seventy, less than a seventh of the whole number, are really of American origin and now in respectable use. As examples may be cited — *backwoodsman, barbecue, belittle, bookstore, bottomlands, breadstuff, caucus, clapboard, creek* in the sense of brook or small stream, *declension* of an office, *deed* as a verb, *desk* for pulpit, *dutiable,* to *girdle* a tree, *gubernatorial, hominy, intervale, salt-lick, lot* — a division of land, *lumber, offset, pine barrens, portage, rapids, renewedly, samp, section* of the country, *sleigh, span* of horses, and *staging* for scaffolding. The other six-sevenths of the book consists of, first, mere vulgarisms and blunders; second, unauthorized expressions invented by eccentric writers and never generally adopted; and, third, words really British in their origin though not current in good London society — to which last class, by the way, it is highly probable that several of the terms above mentioned as genuine Americanisms might be transferred, were their full history known.

VIII.

NOAH WEBSTER'S " LETTER TO THE HONORABLE JOHN PICKERING on the subject of his Vocabulary" is a duodecimo of sixty pages, dated "Dec. 1816." The lexicographer regarded himself, or the principles that he taught, as at least indirectly attacked by the Vocabulary without necessity or reason. As for Mr. Pickering's apprehension that American speech might become in time so depraved that English authors could not be read in this country without translation, he says he " might oppose to this supposition another, which is nearly as probable, that the rivers in America will turn their courses, and flow from the sea to the tops of the hills." Whatever change may be taking place, moreover, he thinks it quite vain to attempt to stop, especially as changes are occurring in England as well: "You take some pains," he says, " to ascertain the point, whether the people of this country now speak and write the English language with purity. The result is, that we have, in several instances, departed from the standard of the language, as spoken and written in England at the present day. Be it so — it is equally true, that the English have departed from the standard, as it appears in the works of Addison. And this is acknowledged by yourself. It is equally true that Addison, Pope and Johnson deviated from the standard of the age of Elizabeth. Now, sir, where is the remedy?" Wherever else it may lie — if remedy is desirable or possible — it certainly does not lie, Dr. Webster thought, in a slavish imitation of British practices. "With regard to the general principle that we must use only such words as the English use," he proceeds, " let me repeat, that the restriction is, in the nature of the thing, impracticable, and the demand that we should observe it, is as improper as it is arrogant. Equally impertinent is it to ridicule us for retaining the use of genuine English words, because they happen to be obsolete in London, or in the higher circles of life. There are many instances in which we retain the genuine use of words, and the genuine English pronunciation, which they have corrupted; in pronunciation they have introduced more corruptions, within half a century, than were ever before introduced in five centuries, not even excepting the periods of conquest. Many of these changes in England are attributable to false principles, introduced into popular elementary books written by mere sciolists in language, and diffused by the instrumentality of the stage. Let the English remove the beam from their own eye, before they attempt to pull the mote from ours; and before they laugh at our vulgar *keow, geown, neow*, let them discard their polite *keind*, and *geuide;* a fault precisely similar in origin, and equally a perversion of genuine English pronunciation." Brave and sensible words are these; their teaching may well be laid to heart to-day!

IX.

DR. ELWYN'S GLOSSARY OF SUPPOSED AMERI-
CANISMS was undertaken, as the preface informs
us, " to show how much there yet remains, in
this country, of language and customs directly
brought from our remotest ancestry " — a purpose quite different from that of Mr. Pickering;
but the chief value of the book is in the contribution it makes to our knowledge of Pennsylvania provincialisms, of which the author is
evidently a careful observer. About four hundred and sixty words are included, of which a
clear majority would be quite as little understood in decent American as in decent British
society; but it seems that we have been accused
of manufacturing the whole list, while the fact is
that they are one and all of foreign origin. The
book is carelessly written, and not accurately
alphabetized.

X.

SCHELE DE VERE'S " AMERICANISMS," a small
octavo of something less than seven hundred

pages, differs from the other works mentioned in not adopting the dictionary form, but presenting our verbal peculiarities as arranged in various classes — those invented by the Indian, the Dutchman, the Frenchman, the Spaniard, the German, the Negro, and the Chinaman; expressions peculiar to the West, to the church, to politics and to trade; marine and railroad terms; cant and slang; new words and nicknames, etc. The author has been accused of plagiarizing from Bartlett, and doubtless did avail himself freely of the labors of that diligent lexicographer; but he added a good deal of original matter, and his book possesses an interest of its own, being indeed the only one of the seven (except perhaps Webster's) that is likely to be read entirely through. About four thousand items appear in the index.

XI.

BARTLETT'S DICTIONARY (or, to give the full title, " Dictionary of Americanisms, a Glossary of Words and Phrases usually regarded as peculiar to the United States, by John Russell Bartlett,") is, in its latest edition, a bulky octavo

of over eight hundred pages, exceedingly well
printed, and containing something above five
thousand six hundred entries, but hardly representing, I think, more than about four hundred
and fifty genuine and distinct Americanisms now
in respectable use — less than one-twelfth of the
whole number of articles. Of the remainder,
nearly four hundred words and phrases are set
down by the author himself as of British origin,
some being used in this country in exactly the
same manner as on their native soil, while others
have been slightly altered in meaning, application or sound.   At least three hundred and
thirty more — and probably a much larger number — are also certainly British, though Mr.
Bartlett seems not to be aware of it. The rest
of the dictionary — say four-fifths — is made up,
partly of expressions never in general use, or
long since antiquated; partly of mere mispro-
nunciations, grammatical errors and unauthorized contractions; partly of vulgar and disgust-
ing slang; and partly of wearisome repetitions.
Yet I by no means desire to be understood as
setting down the work for a mass of rubbish.
On the contrary, it contains a vast fund of inter-

esting and curious information, which any man devoted to the study of English dialects might well be proud to have brought together. Only it is a great pity that the diligent compiler, in his anxiety to make a big book, allowed himself such extreme latitude in his conception of what constitutes an Americanism in speech, and consequently buried his grains of wheat under so appalling a mountain of chaff.

It may be worth while to present some samples of the words that are improperly included in Bartlett's Dictionary, as showing the way in which a tremendous number of pseudo-Americanisms have been, first and last, accumulated by people who find satisfaction in counting them up.

Of the three hundred and eighty-five words and phrases that the author himself sets down as of British origin, the following examples may be mentioned:

To beat one *all-to-pieces*, or *all-to-smash; allow*, for assert; *argufy; awfully*, for very; *bail*, the handle of a bucket; *barm*, for yeast; *bound*, for determined or resolved; a *bull*, on the stock exchange; *bumptious*, for self-conceited; *can't come it; cap sheaf;*

cheek, for impudence; *chowder; clip*, a blow, as,
" he hit him a clip ; " to *collide ;* to *cotton to* a man;
cracker, for a small biscuit; *cute ;* to *cut stick ;* a
deck of cards; *deputize ; doxologize ; dreadful*, for
very, as " dreadful " fine; *every once in a while ;*
fall of the year; *first-rate ; fix*, to put in order;
flapjack ; flummux ; freshet ; gallivant ; galoshes ;
given name ; goodies ; to *gulp ; hand-running ; hard*
up ; heft, for weight; *help*, for servants; *homely*, not
handsome; *hook*, to steal; *immigration ; jeopardize ;*
julep ; to *keep company ;* to *loan ; mad*, for angry;
mighty, for very; *old fogy ; over the left; pair* of
stairs; *pled*, for pleaded; *pry*, a lever; to *pull up*
stakes ; to *reckon*, meaning to think, believe or suppose; *reliable ; rooster ; no great shakes ; sopho-*
more ; spell of weather; *spry; spunk ; starvation ;*
stricken, for struck; *sundown ; swap ;* to *take on ;*
talented ; teetotaller ; ugly, for ill-tempered; to *wal-*
lop, and to *whale ; whapper ;* to *whittle*, and to *wilt.*
In many cases no reason whatever is assigned for
including these words in a list of Americanisms;
very seldom is any better cause mentioned than that
they are provincial or antiquated in Great Britain;
and sometimes the pretext is of the most trivial
character, as in the case of the word *whittle*, which
is put in, forsooth, because both the verb and the
practice are thought to be more common in America

than in England! But the most surprising instance among this class of words has yet to be mentioned — the use of the adverb " *immediately*," in place of the phrase " as soon as " — " the deer fell dead immediately they shot him." This wretched expression, Mr. Bartlett writes, is creeping into use from England. What possible sense there can be in counting as an Americanism a villanously ungrammatical construction which is "creeping into use in this country from England," it would puzzle Fitzedward Hall himself to explain.

Among words and phrases erroneously supposed by Mr. Bartlett to be peculiar to this country, the following have been pointed out by various reviewers of the dictionary:

Baggage; bender, a spree; *blackberry; blow,* to brag; *bluff,* a high bank; to *do a thing brown; bug,* as a general term; *bureau,* a chest of drawers; *catamount; choker,* a cravat; *chore; crevasse; cunning,* in the sense of small and pretty; *educational; eelgrass;* to *egg on; engineer* of a locomotive; *every which way; expect,* for suppose; *fast,* for dissipated; *fellowship,* as a verb; *female,* for woman; *first-class;* to *go to the bad;* to *go gunning; in a horn,* meaning "over the left;" *kink,* an accidental knot or twist; the whole *kit* of them; *muss*, a state of confusion; *notions*, small wares or trifles; *railroad*, as the equivalent of railway; *sappy*, meaning silly; *slosh*, soft mud; *smack*, a blow; *splurge; spree; swingletree;* a *good time;* and *tiptop.*

To these may be added (among many others) the following, which I believe no previous reviewer has noted:

Account — In phrase "of no account" = no importance. The exact phrase will be found in Dickens' Uncommercial Traveler, chap. 6.

Airy — Conceited. This may be found in "Albion's England," by one Warner, published in the mother country in 1606.

All-fired. — Set down as a British provincialism by a writer in Macmillan's Magazine, vol. 5, p. 244.

Alley — A child's marble. So used by Defoe in 1720.

Allspice. — Dates back at least to Burton's Anatomy of Melancholy, 1621.

Ampersand — The short character for the word *and.* This is found in Halliwell.

Appointable. — Used by Foxe, 1563.

Back out. — A natural combination of words hardly deserving place among any sort of isms. It may be found in Scott's Rob Roy, published 1818.

Backward—Bashful. So used in Swift's Tale of a Tub, 1704.

Baggage — A traveller's impedimenta. Repeatedly so used by Shakspeare.

Baiting— Luncheon. Is in the Promptorium Parvulorum, fifteenth century.

Balk — Said of a horse. Traced back in England to the fifteenth century.

Bang up — Superior. American origin very doubtful. Occurs in " Rejected Addresses," 1812.

Bark —To girdle a tree. Used by Shakspeare in Henry VIII.

Beef, an ox, and *Blaze*, a mark on a tree, are both in Halliwell.

Beliked. — Traced back in England to 1557.

Belongings. — Possibly of American origin, but was certainly used in England in 1817.

Bilberry — A plant. Merry Wives of Windsor, V. 5.

Bilk — A cheat. Used by Marvell, 1672.

Bindweed. — Mentioned in Turner's " Names of Herbes," 1548.

Blue-blooded— May be of American origin, but seems to be pretty well naturalized abroad, as Maria Edgeworth uses it in " Helen," 1834.

Bluefish. — Phil. Trans. XXXVIII. 318 (A. D. 1734).

Boo-hoo. — Used by Skelton, 1525.

Bowling Alley. — Occurs, according to Murray, in British laws of the sixteenth century.

Bright — Intelligent. Occurs in Macbeth.

Brummagen — Spurious. A contemptuous phrase "Brummagen Protestants" was in use in England in 1681.

Bully — Fine. Chetham's "Angler's Vade-Mecum," 1681.

By and Large. Found in Sturmy's Mariner's Magazine, 1669.

Caboose (of a freight train). Practically the same use as that defined in Falconer's Marine Dictionary of 1769 — "a sort of house which somewhat resembles a sentry box."

Carry on — To frolic. Certainly well naturalized abroad. Is found in "Dr. Jekyl and Mr. Hyde."

Chance — To risk. Now used in Great Britain. A vulgarism ; but not an Americanism.

Chess — A weed. Used by very old writers on agriculture in England.

Chipper — Lively. Provincial in the Isle of Wight.

Clever, in the sense of good-natured. This is in Halliwell — said to be provincial in the south of England.

Connection, in the phrase "*in this connection.*" Used in Great Britain certainly as long ago as 1780.

Cookey — A little cake. In Prof. J. F. W. Johnston's "Notes on North America," chap. 23, vol. 2, p.

296, we read that this word is familiar to a Scotchman's ears.

Cradle Scythe is in Halliwell.

Firedogs — Andirons. This is found in Brockett's Glossary of North-Country Words.

Hulking (unwieldly), *Jack-at-a-pinch*, and *Pitchin*, are all in Halliwell.

Hunk — A large piece. Provincial in the Isle of Wight.

Right for *very*. Fancy setting this down as an Americanism ! Did Mr. Bartlett ever hear of a Right Honorable minister of Great Britain, or ever read the 139th Psalm — " Marvellous are thy works, and that my soul knoweth right well "?

To *set to rights*. This is said by Elwyn to be an Essex provincialism.

Safe — A place of security. This also is in Elwyn, and said to be from Suffolk.

Sauce — Impudence. This is in Halliwell.

Shinny — A boy's game. This is in Brockett.

Span, for *perfectly*. The expression " span new " is as old as Chaucer.

Stand, a platform, and *Stock*, equivalent to *cattle*, are both in Halliwell.

Stop for *stay*, as " I am stopping at a hotel." The insertion of this detestable Briticism in a dictionary of Americanisms, of all places in the world, is one of the

absurdities of the book.   Everybody who knows anything about the variations of the language as spoken
in the two countries knows that it is heard a thousand
times in England for once that it is noticed here.

Square—Honest.   Shakspeare —Timon of Athens,
V. 5 ; Antony and Cleopatra, II. 2.

Too thin.   Here is another Americanism of a very
remarkable kind.   Smollett was guilty of it, for he
wrote, in " Peregrine Pickle " (published 1751), chap.
26 : " This pretext was too thin to impose upon her
lover."   And Shakspeare, a century and more earlier,
in Henry VIII., Act 5, Scene 2, makes the king say :
" You were ever good at sudden commendations,
Bishop of Winchester.   But know I come not to hear
such flattery now, and in my presence ; they are too
thin and base to hide offences."   Other instances
could no doubt be found in plenty, if it were worth
while to look for them.   But when one considers
that the phrase is invariably applied — as Smollett
applies it — to *pretexts*, coverings, what can be more
obvious than that it must necessarily always have
been, not only perfectly good English, but the simplest and most natural expression imaginable?   The
insertion of a phrase like that in a list of Americanisms or any other sort of isms, only shows what follies
men may be led into, upon whom the craze for making long compilations has once seized.

Tophet— The place of torment. This familiar Biblical term is of course just as much an Americanism as is *Eden*, or *Babylon*, or *Jerusalem*.

Touch-and-go. Who does not remember the "touch-and-go young Barnacle" of the Circumlocution Office in Charles Dickens' "Little Dorrit"?

Tramp, a strolling vagabond, is in Halliwell.

"*Well*," a meaningless prefix to a sentence. The word is twice used in this way by highly-aristocratic speakers in the first chapter of Beaconsfield's "Endymion." The author would have been slightly amused if Mr. Bartlett had informed him that he represented Sidney Wilton and William Ferrars as conversing in the American dialect.

It would be unprofitable to detail examples of the mere errors, vulgar expressions and slang terms which Mr. Bartlett enumerates as peculiarly American. A few instances of his senseless repetitions, enlarging the book to no possible good, may be mentioned with less disgust:

"Bankit (French Banquette)" is defined as a sidewalk in Louisiana. Immediately below we have "banquette, the name for the sidewalk in some of our southern cities." "Bowie," and "bowie-knife" are separately entered. "Breakbone" is "a species of fever," and then follows " breakbone fever," with full definition. " Bulldoze " is " to intimidate," and on the next page we have "to bulldoze," "to intimidate by violent means." A "filibuster" is a freebooter; "filibustering" is "freebooting;" and "to filibuster" is "to acquire by freebooting;" three separate entries. "A loafer" is an idle lounger, and "to loaf" is "to lounge." "To lynch," "lyncher" and "lynch law" are separately explained. "Muss," a corruption of "mess," is first elaborately defined as a noun, with examples, and then as a verb. A "pony" is a translation, and " to pony " is to use a translation. " To post " a person is to inform him, and then we are told that " posted " means informed. "To red up," meaning to set in order, is twice defined — once on page 517 and again on page 520. "To run" is " to cause to run," with the phrase " to run a church " as an example ; and just below we find another entry — "to run a church," " to have the charge of a church." " To spin street yarn " (page 636) is " to go gadding about the streets;" and on page 798, under the heading " street yarn," we learn that " to spin street yarn " is " to frequent the streets without any definite object." A " stove pipe " is a tall hat; and then follows a second entry, "stove pipe hat, a tall hat." A "suck in " is " a cheat," and " to suck in " is " to take in, to cheat." Many more

To those interested in the

BONNIE BRIER BUSH

Ian Maclaren's First Novel

KATE CARNEGIE

Will Appear in the January

...BOOKMAN

and continue throughout the year.

Important

With the January number the Price of
THE BOOKMAN will be raised to $2.00
per year and 20 cents per number.

All subscribing before January 25 will
receive THE BOOKMAN at the old rate, $1.50.

Send 10 cents for Sample Copy.

- -

DODD, MEAD & CO., 149 Fifth Ave., New York,

will please send the BOOKMAN for...............years

to................................... ....

instances might be mentioned ; but it is hardly necessary to go further than this, in order to show how the book is filled up and expanded, without rhyme or reason. Mr. Bartlett would have done better to take pattern from Halliwell's admirable dictionary, a work that contains nearly ten times as many entries as the Dictionary of Americanisms, but fills less than fifty more pages.

Coming now to genuine Americanisms, words and phrases really peculiar to this country, or used here in a sense never recognized in England, the following are among those which are either omitted by Bartlett or about which he makes statements that seem to invite remark :

Blizzard. — This word Mr. Bartlett defines as "a poser," having noticed, apparently, only a single instance of its use, and jumped at the conclusion that this is the meaning intended. He adds the comment, "not known in the Eastern States," which was generally true, no doubt, until the sharp winter of 1880–'81 familiarized the term — as well as the thing itself, in a greatly modified form — to the residents of the East. I suppose I need not say that a real blizzard, as the word is now understood, is a terrific storm, with low barometer, light clouds or none at all, "and the air full of particles of snow, in the form of dry, sharp crystals, which, driven before the wind, bite and sting like fire." The term is said to have made its first appearance in print about the year 1860, in a newspaper called the Northern Vindicator, published at Estherville, Minn. Its etymology can only be guessed at, but there has been no lack of guesses. The English word *blister;* the French *bouillard* (see Surenne's Dictionary); the German *blitz;* the Spanish *brisa;* the surname *Blizzard* (said to be common around Baltimore); an unpronounceable Sioux term; and the Scotch verb *blizzen*, of which Jamieson's Dictionary remarks that "drought is said to be *blizzening* when the wind parches and withers the fruits of the earth" — all these, and I know not how many other words in different languages, have been suggested, with various degrees of improbability, as the origin of the term. My own conjecture is, that it is simply an onomatopœia; an attempt, not wholly unsuccessful, to represent the whistling and "driving" noise of a terrible storm. It should be added, before leaving this word, that it seems to have been occasionally used in various places in the Eastern States, for a long time past, in significations quite different from its present meaning. Thus a newspaper correspondent writes from Solon, Me., to the effect that twenty or thirty years ago the phrase "let her blizzard" was common in that locality, meaning "let her go," as applied to the act of firing a gun or throwing a stone. Another, living in Perry County, Pa., has heard the word for many years as the equivalent of a drink — "let's take a blizzard." It is said also to have been in use in the same county in its present signification, as early as 1836, but to have become obsolete in this meaning, years ago. A well-informed friend at the West writes me as below: "This word is in common use in Texas, and has been for many years, to describe a very severe 'norther.' It has been stated to me on competent authority that the thermometer has been known to register from, say, 86° down to 26°, the change being effected within the space of six or seven hours ! This has always been popularly known as a blizzard. When the temperature in the summer season would be lowered only say 20°, it was known only as a norther. I think the term has gradually crept northward, until its significance is generally understood west of the Mississippi."

Bogus. — This word is older than the earliest date given by Bartlett, June 12, 1857; it was used in the Painesville (O.) Telegraph of July 6, 1827. Also the etymology which he gives (a corruption of *Borghese*) is not certain. It is said (by the Augusta, Ga., Chronicle) to be from the name of one William

A. Bogus, "a Georgia land lottery commissioner, caught in rascality, an issuer of fraudulent land rights;" and it has been conjectured to be a variant of *bagasse* (sugar-cane refuse), or an abbreviation of *tantrabogus,* said to be old Vermont slang for any object of evil appearance.

Boom — A semi-slang expression (which first appeared in the 1881 supplement to Worcester) descriptive of a sudden advance in popularity or in price. Said to be borrowed from the mining phraseology of the far West, where a process called "booming" is sometimes adopted to clear off surface soil and reveal supposed mineral veins. An artificial reservoir is constructed near the summit of a mountain, which is first allowed to fill with water and is then suddenly opened, whereupon a terrific torrent rushes down the slope, carrying rocks, trees, earth and all, with resistless force. A newspaper writer says he has "seen gullies fifty, seventy-five, and in some places a hundred feet deep, and extending the whole length of the mountain," cut out by single booms. "The word booming," he adds, "has therefore a very significant meaning, and is expressive as a word phrase, for it denotes an overwhelming, irresistible power and force."

To *buck against* — To oppose violently. I suppose this verb to be of American invention.

Canaille — Shorts, or low grades of flour; so defined in the Worcester Supplement, where it is said to be common in Canada and New England.

Casket — A kind of coffin. This first appeared in the Webster Supplement of 1879.

Coal. Bartlett blunders fearfully in attempting to give the names of the different sizes of coal. His list is: 1, Broken or furnace coal, being the largest lumps; 2, Stove or range; 3, Pea or nut; 4, Egg; 5, Coal dust. I believe the correct nomenclature is: 1, Furnace; 2, Egg; 3, Stove; 4, Chestnut; 5, Pea; 6, Buckwheat; 7, Coal dust.

Coral of lobster — Unimpregnated eggs; first appeared (incorrectly defined) in the Webster Supplement.

Dodger — A small hand-bill; first defined in the Century Dictionary.

Escalan — Twelve and a-half cents, a New Orleans term not in the dictionaries.

Fair — An exhibition, not primarily for the purpose of sale. This very common American use of the word was not recognized by any dictionary in common use until the publication, in March, 1890, of the second volume of the Century. Long before that date, however, it had passed into very respectable British use — see for instance the Westminster Review for October, 1881 — No. 230, p. 247.

Fakir — First a magician, then a showman with a worthless exhibit, lastly a cheat. These applications of the term appear to be of American origin, as are the derivative *fake* (noun and verb) and the altered spelling *faker*.

French — A term used in Maryland and Virginia for anything that is greatly disliked. " For instance," says a writer, " the tobacco gets the worm in it that destroys it; they call in ' frenching.' And if the children have the measles very bad, it is ' French,' and the same with a bad case of small-pox — it is the ' real French small-pox.' "

Furore — An excitement; first noticed in the Century. Bartlett overlooked it, though it appears in one of his citations, under the heading " Nick."

Gripsack — A recently-invented and rather vulgar term for a satchel, chiefly heard, I believe, at the West.

Handglass. Bartlett says handglasses are spectacles. My impression is that the term generally denotes a small looking-glass.

Highwines. I am not certain that this is an American coinage, but I believe it appears in no dictionary except the Worcester Supplement.

Institute — A convention. Farmers' institutes — meetings lasting two or three days, with lectures and discussions, are very common.

Keet. Bartlett says "Guinea keets" are Guinea fowls. I think the "keets" are Guinea *eggs* — so called at the West. See Milwaukee *Republican-Sentinel*, Dec. 7, 1882, (No. 12,551,) second page, second column.

Listing — A method of planting corn; see Cultivator & Country Gentleman, vol. 49, p. 187.

Mugwump. Introduced into common use since Bartlett published. First defined in the Webster International of 1890.

Mung news. Bartlett says this means false news. I have never heard the word; but a writer in Blackwood's Edinburgh Magazine for October, 1877, says it is the preterite of the old English verb *ming*, to mix — whence *mingle* — and means, not false, but confused, mingled, mixed up.

You *must not*, as the reverse of you *may*. I am inclined to think this is an Americanism, as I judge that the English generally say "you may not" — in which, if so, they are certainly more logical than we. "You must" means that an obligation rests upon you; therefore "you must not," ought to mean merely that there is no obligation. "You may," means that permission is granted, and therefore when permission is withheld and the action prohibited, the phrase ought to be "you may not," instead of the universal American practice of saying "you must not."

Closely allied to this, is the incorrect use of *can* for *may*, where there is no question of ability — which seems to be rather more prevalent in this country than in England. A line on the face of our postal-cards formerly made the statement that "nothing but the address can be placed on this side." The possessor of the card *can* place there any number of words that there is room for, if he pleases. What is meant is, of course, that nothing but the address *may* be placed there ; that is, it is forbidden to place there anything else, under penalty of forfeiting the privilege of sending the card by mail. The English newspaper wrappers have a similar notice, correctly worded : "This wrapper *may* only be used for newspapers, or for such documents as are allowed to be sent at the book-rate."

Ninepence — Twelve and a-half cents. Formerly used in New England and Virginia.

Pit — The stone of a fruit. " Mostly confined to New York State," Bartlett says. I think the term is now common at the West, and used to some extent in the South, at least in Alabama.

Railroad Nomenclature. Bartlett gives a list of eighteen objects pertaining to railroads, which have different names in the two countries ; but fails to note that the American " buffer " is the English " bumper," and the American " grade " the English " gradient."

Round-up — An annual collection of cattle on the plains of the West, for branding and other purposes. Perhaps from Spanish *rodear*, to encompass.

Sheeny. This means, Bartlett says, " a sharp fellow." I think it is a cant term for a Jew, entirely irrespective of his character.

Smitch — A very small quantity of anything. This word is noted by a writer in Lippincott's Magazine for March, 1869, as peculiar to Carbon County, Pa. I have heard it in Albany.

Solid-colored — All of the same color. This expression, very common among breeders of Jersey cattle, and also used, I believe, in the dry-goods trade, may not be an Americanism perhaps, but no British dictionary defines it.

Super. Bartlett says this is a contraction of " superintendent of factories, theatres," etc. What the " super " of a factory may be, if there is an official so called, I do not know; but the " super," or, as he is commonly called, the " supe " at a theatre, is certainly by no means a superintendent, but a supernumerary.

Sweeny — A kind of muscular atrophy in horses. First defined in Webster International, though an old word. It may be found in the Cultivator of October, 1843, p. 166, and in Jennings' " Horse and his Diseases," copyrighted 1860, p. 297.

Tenderfoot — A new arrival from civilization in the wild regions of the far West; see Scribner's Monthly, vol. 18, p. 815.   Noticed in Webster International.

Trousers — Equivalent of *pantalets;* see Harper's Magazine, May, 1851, p. 864.   Perhaps not an Americanism, but the dictionaries define *trousers* as a garment for males only.

Whiskey.   It is perhaps to Mr. Bartlett's credit that he does not seem to be very well "up" on the varieties of this popular beverage, as he remarks that "Bourbon whiskey is the best, being made of rye." As to the question of Bourbon's being the best, there may be differences of opinion; our Scotch and Irish friends, to say nothing of others, would perhaps dissent from the lexicographer's judgment; but as to Bourbon's being made of rye, we must all take exception to that statement, the fact being, I believe, that Bourbon never contains more than one-third of rye, and seldom as much as that.

To these genuine Americanisms may be added a few scientific or pseudo-scientific words, such as *phonograph, photophone, audiphone* and *lysimeter. Telephone*, as may not be generally known, is, like *telegraph*, much older than the apparatus that we now call by these terms; the original telegraph was a semaphore, and the original telephone, I believe, a speaking trumpet. And if time permitted, and the game were worth the candle, a numerous list of curious names of places, of American invention, might be compiled from the Post-Office Directory. Mr. Bartlett has done something at this, in his preface; but he failed to notice Why Not, Autumn Leaves, Bird-in-Hand and Youngwomanstown, Pa.; Bogus, Fiddletown, Hay Fork, Port Wine and Yankee Jim's, Cal.; Nola Chucky, Jim Ned, Mouse Tail, A. B. C. and U Bet, Tenn.; Long Year and The Corner, N. Y.; Hash Knife and Mud Creek, Texas; Star of the West, Sub Rosa and Gum Log, Ark.; Non Intervention, Va.; Quashquetown, Iowa; Medybemps, Me.; Rooster Rock, Oregon; Look Out, Dak.; Rabbit Hash, Ky.; Ty Ty, Geo.; Zig, Mo.; Skull Valley, Ariz.; Greenhorn, Left Hand, Ni Wot and O. Z., Col.; T. B., Md., and scores of other oddities that might be mentioned. It is a thousand pities that we have not preserved a greater number of the more euphonious geographical names of the aborigines; and it is to be sincerely hoped that as refinement and good taste become more general, we shall by degrees weed out most of these rough-and-ready appellations.

XII.

Mr. John S. Farmer's work, "American-isms Old and New," is a "foolscap quarto" of about 590 pages, "privately printed" in what is intended to be a very ornamental (but is not a very tasteful) style, elaborately bound, and sold at a high price to subscribers only, each copy being signed and numbered. It is unique in being the production, not only of an Englishman, but of an Englishman who seems never to have visited the United States, and whose ideas of our geography and history are of the vaguest description. He calls this country " the future mighty commonwealth of the southern seas " (p. ix.), counts Maine and Vermont among the original thirteen (p. 221), and names "Virginia, North-Carolina, South-Carolina, Georgia " —these four only — as the Southern States (p. 506). Innumerable minor blunders are therefore not surprising — such for example as the statement that "under the rigid Wall Street rules every transaction is an actual purchase

and sale of actual stock; the broker who sells
one hundred shares of Erie actually delivers to
the purchaser the certificate of stock issued by
the company" (p. 93). Elsewhere we read
that the term *bulldoze* originally referred " to an
association *of negroes* formed to insure, by violent and unlawful means, the success of an
election " (p. 100); that spelling bees originated
in the Western States (p. 507); that *bank bill* is
"the name by which *Bank of England* notes are
generally known throughout the States;" that
bubby is " a pet name for a baby " (p. 91); that
a *freezer* is a refrigerator (p. 254); that " previous to 1878 *greenbacks* for amounts down to ten
cents were current," and that " *Greenbackers* were
those who, previous to the resumption of specie
payment for the smaller amount just named,
opposed the change " (p. 276); that *huckleberry*
is " a kind of blackberry " (p. 308); that *jag*
is " a slang term for an umbrella" (p. 321);
that " *may-be* is invariably used for *perhaps* "
(p. 361); that " a cent piece" is " made of nickel"
(p. 389); that the Northwestern States are Ohio,
Indiana, Illinois, Michigan, Wisconsin, Minne-
sota, Iowa and Nebraska (p. 393); that poker is

"as universally played in America as is whist in England" (p. 429); that a *sack coat* is "a tweed cloth coat" (p. 468); that a *sarcophagus* is "a leaden coffin" (p. 471); and that a *stateroom* on a steamer is "the cabin" (p. 515). The book is in fact utterly useless as a source of information; no reliance can be placed on any statement made in its pages. Credit should nevertheless be given to Mr. Farmer for his entire freedom from the insular superciliousness that one might naturally expect to find him combining with his ignorance of the United States. He is studiously courteous as well as fair; and he goes out of his way to remark (p. 48) that "American English, taking the people all round, is much purer than the vernacular of the mother country." On the whole, therefore, and considering the fund of amusement that his "portentous catch-guinea" (as the New York Post called the book on its appearance) is certain to afford them, Americans have every reason to be grateful to Mr. Farmer, and to wish him well Would that all our British critics possessed the same elementary qualification for discussing the peculiarities of the American language!

XIII.

COL. NORTON'S "POLITICAL AMERICAN-ISMS" contains some 350 entries — among which it is a little surprising to find *boycott,* " an adaptation from the Irish Nationalists, with the same general meaning." An occasional slip — such as the statements that the term *half-breed* was "originally applied to certain Republicans of New-York who *wavered in their party allegiance* during a bitter contest over the U. S. senatorship in 1881," and that "every Democratic newspaper has a cut of a ' rooster' in the act of crowing," which "is invariably printed at the head of a column announcing a party victory" — will be noted by the critical reader; but the work is on the whole remarkably well done and likely to prove serviceable. It belongs of course to rather a different class from that of the preceding treatises on Americanisms, and hardly calls for extended review.

BIBLIOGRAPHY.

———◆———

I. Books entirely Devoted to " Americanisms."

1. A Vocabulary, or Collection of Words and Phrases which have been supposed to be peculiar to the United States, to which is prefixed an Essay on the Present State of the English Language in the United States. By John Pickering. Boston; Cummings & Hilliard, 1816; 8vo.; pp. 208.

2. Letter to the Hon. John Pickering, on the subject of his Vocabulary. By Noah Webster. Boston; West & Richardson, 1817; small 8vo. ; pp. 60.

3. Glossary of Supposed Americanisms, collected by Alfred L. Elwyn, M. D. Philadelphia; J. B. Lippincott & Co., 1859; 12mo.; pp. 122.

4. Americanisms; the English of the New World. By M. Schele de Vere, LL. D. New York ; Charles Scribner & Co., 1872; 8vo.; pp. 686.

5. Dictionary of Americanisms; a Glossary of Words and Phrases usually regarded as peculiar to the United States. By John Russell Bartlett. Fourth edition. Boston; Little, Brown & Co., 1877; 8vo.; pp. 814.

6. AMERICANISMS, Old and New, a Dictionary of Words, Phrases and Colloquialisms peculiar to the United States, British America, the West Indies, etc., etc., their Derivation, Meaning and Application, together with numerous Anecdotal, Historical, Explanatory and Folk-Lore Notes. Compiled and edited by JOHN S. FARMER. London; Thos. Poulter & Sons, 1889; "foolscap 4to."; pp. 564.

7. POLITICAL AMERICANISMS; a Glossary of Terms and Phrases current at different periods in American Politics. By CHARLES LEDYARD NORTON. New York; Longmans, Green & Co., 1890; 16mo.; pp. 134.

II. CHAPTERS OR PARTS OF BOOKS.

1. JOHN WITHERSPOON, D. D. Essays on Americanisms, Perversions of Language in the United States, Cant Phrases, etc., in 4th vol. of his works, published in 8vo., Philadelphia, 1801. (The earliest work on American vulgarisms. Originally published as a series of essays, entitled "The Druid," which appeared in a periodical in 1761.)

2. ADIEL SHERWOOD. Gazetteer of Georgia. Charleston, 1827; Philadelphia, 1829; Washington, 1837. Has glossary of slang and vulgar words used in the Southern States.

3. T. ROMEYN BECK, M. D., LL. D. "Notes on Pickering's Vocabulary." Albany Institute Transactions, Vol. I., p. 25; Albany, N. Y., 1830.

4. JAMES RUSSELL LOWELL. Biglow Papers, 1848, 1864. Introductions to First and Second Series, and Glossary.

5. CHARLES ASTOR BRISTED. " The English Language in America," in Cambridge Essays. London ; John W. Parker & Son, 1855. (Shows " rare " meat, and " corned " for *drunk*, to be expressions of English origin.)

6. W. C. FOWLER, LL. D. English Grammar. New York; Harper & Bros., 1855, 8vo.; pp. 119-129. Also 12mo., 1858; pp. 23-27.

7. GEORGE P. MARSH. Lectures on the English Language. Fourth edition; New York; Charles Scribner's Sons, 1859. Lecture 30, " The English Language in America."

8. G. F. GRAHAM. A Book about Words ; London ; Longmans, Green & Co., 1869 ; chap. 13, " Slang Words and Americanisms."

9. R. G WHITE. Words and Their Uses ; New York ; Sheldon & Co., 1870 ; chap. 3, " British-English and American-English." Also, Every-day English ; Boston ; Houghton, Mifflin & Co., 1880 ; chap. 6, " American Speech."

10. Prof. W. D. WHITNEY. Language and the Study of Language, 5th edition ; New York ; Charles Scribner & Co., 1870 ; pp. 171-174.

11. G. C. EGGLESTON. A Man of Honor ; New York ; Orange Judd Co., 1873. (Illustrates various Virginia provincialisms.)

12. A. J. ELLIS. Early English Pronunciation ; London ; Trübner & Co., 1874. Part 4, pp. 1217-'30. (In-

cludes considerable notice of pronunciation used by American humorists.)

13. G. A. BARRINGER. "*Etude sur l'Anglais parlé aux Etats Unis* (*La Langue Americaine*)," in *Actes de la Société Philologique de Paris*, March, 1874. (Largely transferred from De Vere.)

14. GILBERT M. TUCKER. "American English." Albany Institute Transactions, Vol. X. p. 334; Albany, N. Y., 1883.

15. Rev. Dr. SAMUEL FALLOWS. Synonyms and Antonyms; New York; F. H. Revell, 1886 ; pp. 294–342. "Dictionary of Americanisms, Briticisms, etc."

16. R. O. WILLIAMS. Our Dictionaries; New York; Henry Holt & Co., 1890; pp. 71–128.

17. BRANDER MATTHEWS. Americanisms and Briticisms ; New York ; Harper & Bros., 1892 ; pp. 1–59.

18. Various Encyclopedias — the Americana, Appleton's, Chambers', Library of Universal Knowledge, etc. Article, "Americanisms."

19. Worcester's Dictionary, ed. 1881, p. *l.*

III. ARTICLES IN BRITISH PERIODICALS.

[The figures at the left of the decimal point indicate the volume ; those at the right, the page.]

BLACKWOOD'S EDINBURGH MAGAZINE: 89.421 ; 102.399 ("Inroads upon English.")

CHAMBERS' JOURNAL : Dec. 20, 1873, p. 801 ; March 31,

1875, p. 171 ("American Nicknames"); Sept. 25,
1875, p. 609; Jan. 30, 1886, p. 70.

CORNHILL MAGAZINE: 58.363.

ECLECTIC REVIEW: (N. S.) 13.356 — April, 1820 (Review of Pickering).

ILLUSTRATED LONDON NEWS: 82.87 (G. A. Sala, Review of Tucker in North-American Review); 84.339 (Sala, Review of Tucker in Albany Institute Transactions); 84.543 (Sala, Reply to Smalley in N. Y. Tribune).

KNOWLEDGE: 6.319; 8.171; 9.159, 178, 196, 249, 275, 332, 352; 10.14, 38, 41, 66, 113, 183, 230, 274; 11.28, 82, 129, 183, 223.

LEISURE HOUR: 26.110; 36.827.

LONGMANS' MAGAZINE: 1.80 ("Some Points in American Speech and Customs," by E. A. Freeman).

NINETEENTH CENTURY, September, 1880. ("English, Rational and Irrational," by Fitzedward Hall.)

PENNY MAGAZINE: July 21, 1838, p. 278. (Severe on American Speech.)

QUARTERLY REVIEW: 10.528.

SATURDAY REVIEW: 60.709 (Review of "Political Americanisms" in Mag. of Am. Hist.); 62.142; 62.190.

SPECTATOR: 62.493 (Review of Farmer).

WESTMINSTER REVIEW: 130.35 (no dialects in United States); No. 234, Oct., 1882, p. 279, Scott edition (admits that the English call *now* "*nao*").

IV. Articles in American Periodicals.

Analectic Magazine: 3.404. (Sarcastic [?] defense of American freedom of speech; recommends invention of a new language.)

Appletons' Journal : (N. S.) 11.315. ("English and American-English," by Richard A. Proctor, from Gentleman's Magazine — copied also, in part, in N. Y. *Tribune*, Aug. 14, 1881.)

Atlantic Monthly: 6.667; 40.233; 41.495 (R. G. White, Review of Bartlett); 41.656 (do.) ; 42.97 (do.); 42.342 (do.) ; 42.619 (do.) ; 42.643 (Reply to White); 43.88 (White on Bartlett); 43.109 (freight train and spool) ; 43.379 (White on Bartlett)'; 43.656 (do.) ; 44.654 (White, "Assorted Americanisms") ; 45.428 (Reply to White); 45.669 (White, "British Americanisms") ; 47.697 (White, supplementary to Bartlett articles) ; 48.849; 52.792; 53.286; 53.290; 55.593 (R. A. Proctor, "The Misused H of England") ; 55.856 (right away).

Buffalo Commercial Advertiser: Sept. 10–11, 1888. (Article on pronunciation, from Critic.)

Canadian Monthly: 1.87. (Review of De Vere)

Century: 47(25).848 ("Wild Flowers of English Speech in America," by Edward Eggleston); 48-(26).867 ("Folk Speech in America," by Edward Eggleston).

Chicago News: March 10, 1890. (London Letter from Eugene Field.)

Critic : 13.97, 104, 115, 263.

FORUM: 2.117. ("Americanisms in England," by A. C. Coxe.)

GALAXY: 21.521 (White, Pronunciation); 24.376 (White on Bartlett); 24.681 (do.).

HARPER'S MONTHLY: 66.665 (Sussex expressions); 83.215 (Brander Matthews, Briticisms and Americanisms); 85.277 (Matthews, American spelling); 90.252 (Shakspeare's Americanisms).

HOURS AT HOME: 5.361 (Review of "Queen's English," by F. W. Shelton).

INTERNATIONAL REVIEW : 8.472 (" English Language in America," by Lounsbury) ; 8.596 (do.).

LAKESIDE MONTHLY : 3.154.

LIPPINCOTT'S MAGAZINE: 3.310 (Provincialisms, by Henry Reeves) ; 4.345 ; 5.545 (by N. S. Dodge); 19.513; 31.378 (Review of Freeman in Longmans'), 44.121 (mugwump).

LITERARY WORLD: 14.364.

LITTELL'S LIVING AGE: 20.79 (Review of Bartlett, from Boston *Advertiser*) ; 95.218 (" Inroads upon English," from Blackwood. as above); 100.636 (Review of Zincke's " Last Winter in the United States," from Spectator); 114.446; 120.240 (" United States English," from Chambers' Journal); 132.821 (from Leisure Hour) ; 155.483 (Freeman's Longmans' article) ; 179.298 (The Great American Language, from Cornhill Magazine).

MAGAZINE OF AMERICAN HISTORY: 12.564 (C. L. Norton, Political Americanisms) ; 13.98 (do.) ; 13.-199 (do.) ; 13.295 (do.) ; 13.394(do.) ; 13.495 (do.) ; 13.599 (comments on foregoing).

NATION : 5.428; 6.392 ; 11.56 (Pennsylvania provincialisms); 11.72 (do.) ; 14.28 (Savage Review of De Vere); 14.45 (Review of Hoosier Schoolmaster) ; 16.148 (North Carolina provincialisms) ; 16.183 (do.) ; 17.113 (Words from Indian languages); 18.380 (Review of Barringer) ; 21.8 (Penn. pro.); 26.171 (Review of Bartlett) ; 26.243 (Review of Bartlett) ; 32.184 (blizzard) ; 32.208 (do.) ; 32.220 (do.) ; 32.260 (do.) ; 49.15 (Review of Farmer).

NATIONAL QUARTERLY REVIEW : 2.230 (Review of Pickering and Bartlett).

NEW ENGLAND MAGAZINE : 6.583 (shows New England provincialisms to be old English).

NEW ENGLANDER : (N. S.) 3.429. (No. 157, July, 1880.)

NEW YORK TRIBUNE: Aug. 14, 1881 (Proctor) ; May 17, 1884 (G. W. Smalley on Sala on Tucker) ; Sept. 29, 1894 (Smalley).

NORTH AMERICAN REVIEW: 3.355 (Review of Pickering) ; 69.94 (Review of Bartlett) ; 91.507 (Review of Marsh's Lectures) ; 136.55 (Tucker, American English) ; 141.431 ("Slang in America," by Walt Whitman) ; 146.709 (lagniappe and brottus); 147.102 (brottus); 147.348 (brottus, buckra, goober); 147.475 (lagniappe and brottus).

PUTNAM'S MONTHLY : 16.519 ("The American Language," by W. W. Crane).

RURAL NEW YORKER : 49.231 (North Carolina provincialisms).

SCRIBNER'S MONTHLY : 3.379 (Review of De Vere).

SOUTHERN LITERARY MESSENGER: 2.110; 14.623 (Review of Bartlett).

SOUTHERN REVIEW: (N. S.) 9.290 and 9.529 ("Americanisms, a Study of Words and Manners"; an elaborate essay, in review of Bartlett's and Webster's dictionaries, and various other books; unduly severe upon American English; author evidently prejudiced).

₊ For other references, see Dialect Notes (Am. Dialect Society, Edward S. Sheldon, secretary, Cambridge, Mass.,) Part I. p. 13, Part II. p. 80, Part V. p. 254.

₊ The author will be greatly obliged for additions or corrections to this list, or to any other part of the book. Instances of the customary use in Great Britain of "American" peculiarities of speech will be especially welcome. Please address at Albany, N. Y.

INDEX.

www.ingramcontent.com/pod-product-compliance
Lightning Source LLC
Chambersburg PA
CBHW030402270326
41926CB00009B/1222